NoLex 1-13

MARC ANTONY

MARC ANTONY

Mary Kittredge

CHELSEA HOUSE PUBLISHERS

NEW YORK

NEW HAVEN   PHILADELPHIA

EDITOR-IN-CHIEF: Nancy Toff
EXECUTIVE EDITOR: Remmel T. Nunn
MANAGING EDITOR: Karyn Gullen Browne
COPY CHIEF: Juliann Barbato
PICTURE EDITOR: Adrian G. Allen
ART DIRECTOR: Giannella Garrett
MANUFACTURING MANAGER: Gerald Levine

Staff for MARC ANTONY:

SENIOR EDITOR: John W. Selfridge
ASSISTANT EDITORS: Sean Dolan, Pierre Hauser, Kathleen McDermott
EDITORIAL ASSISTANT: David Wm. Gibson
COPY EDITORS: Terrance Dolan, Ellen Scordato
ASSOCIATE PICTURE EDITOR: Juliette Dickstein
PICTURE RESEARCHER: Diane Wallis
SENIOR DESIGNER: Debby Jay
ASSISTANT DESIGNER: Jill Goldreyer
PRODUCTION COORDINATOR: Joe Romano
COVER ILLUSTRATION: Carol McDougall

CREATIVE DIRECTOR: Harold Steinberg

The publisher dedicates this book to the memory of Irene Friedman whose contribution to this series was inspiring.

Frontispiece courtesy of Art Resource

3 5 7 9 8 6 4 2

Library of Congress Cataloging in Publication Data

Kittredge, Mary. MARC ANTONY

(World leaders past & present)
Bibliography: p.
Includes index.
1. Antonius, Marcus, 83?–30 B.C.—Juvenile literature.
2. Rome—History—53–44 B.C.—Juvenile literature.
3. Rome—History—Civil War, 43–31 B.C.—Juvenile
literature. 4. Statesmen—Rome—Biography—Juvenile
literature. 5. Generals—Rome—Biography—Juvenile
literature. [1. Antony, Mark, 83?–30 B.C. 2. Statesmen.
3. Generals. 4. Rome—History—53–44 B.C. 5. Rome—
History—Civil War, 43–31 B.C.] I. Title. II. Series: World
leaders past & present.
DG260.A6K57   1988   937'.05'0924 [B] [92]   87-15070

ISBN 0-87754-505-7

Contents

CHELSEA HOUSE PUBLISHERS

WORLD LEADERS PAST & PRESENT

ADENAUER
ALEXANDER THE GREAT
MARC ANTONY
KING ARTHUR
ATATÜRK
ATTLEE
BEGIN
BEN-GURION
BISMARCK
LÉON BLUM
BOLÍVAR
CESARE BORGIA
BRANDT
BREZHNEV
CAESAR
CALVIN
CASTRO
CATHERINE THE GREAT
CHARLEMAGNE
CHIANG KAI-SHEK
CHURCHILL
CLEMENCEAU
CLEOPATRA
CORTÉS
CROMWELL
DANTON
DE GAULLE
DE VALERA
DISRAELI
EISENHOWER
ELEANOR OF AQUITAINE
QUEEN ELIZABETH I
FERDINAND AND ISABELLA
FRANCO

FREDERICK THE GREAT
INDIRA GANDHI
MOHANDAS GANDHI
GARIBALDI
GENGHIS KHAN
GLADSTONE
GORBACHEV
HAMMARSKJÖLD
HENRY VIII
HENRY OF NAVARRE
HINDENBURG
HITLER
HO CHI MINH
HUSSEIN
IVAN THE TERRIBLE
ANDREW JACKSON
JEFFERSON
JOAN OF ARC
POPE JOHN XXIII
LYNDON JOHNSON
JUÁREZ
JOHN F. KENNEDY
KENYATTA
KHOMEINI
KHRUSHCHEV
MARTIN LUTHER KING, JR.
KISSINGER
LENIN
LINCOLN
LLOYD GEORGE
LOUIS XIV
LUTHER
JUDAS MACCABEUS
MAO ZEDONG

MARY, QUEEN OF SCOTS
GOLDA MEIR
METTERNICH
MUSSOLINI
NAPOLEON
NASSER
NEHRU
NERO
NICHOLAS II
NIXON
NKRUMAH
PERICLES
PERÓN
QADDAFI
ROBESPIERRE
ELEANOR ROOSEVELT
FRANKLIN D. ROOSEVELT
THEODORE ROOSEVELT
SADAT
STALIN
SUN YAT-SEN
TAMERLANE
THATCHER
TITO
TROTSKY
TRUDEAU
TRUMAN
VICTORIA
WASHINGTON
WEIZMANN
WOODROW WILSON
XERXES
ZHOU ENLAI

ON LEADERSHIP
Arthur M. Schlesinger, jr.

LEADERSHIP, it may be said, is really what makes the world go round. Love no doubt smooths the passage; but love is a private transaction between consenting adults. Leadership is a public transaction with history. [The idea of leadership affirms the capacity of individuals to move, inspire, and mobilize masses of people so that they act together in pursuit of an end.] Sometimes leadership serves good purposes, sometimes bad; but whether the end is benign or evil, great leaders are those men and women who leave their personal stamp on history.

Now, the very concept of leadership implies the proposition that individuals can make a difference. This proposition has never been universally accepted. From classical times to the present day, eminent thinkers have regarded individuals as no more than the agents and pawns of larger forces, whether the gods and goddesses of the ancient world or, in the modern era, race, class, nation, the dialectic, the will of the people, the spirit of the times, history itself. Against such forces, the individual dwindles into insignificance.

So contends the thesis of historical determinism. Tolstoy's great novel *War and Peace* offers a famous statement of the case. Why, Tolstoy asked, did millions of men in the Napoleonic wars, denying their human feelings and their common sense, move back and forth across Europe slaughtering their fellows? "The war," Tolstoy answered, "was bound to happen simply because it was bound to happen." All prior history predetermined it. As for leaders, they, Tolstoy said, "are but the labels that serve to give a name to an end and, like labels, they have the least possible connection with the event." The greater the leader, "the more conspicuous the inevitability and the predestination of every act he commits." The leader, said Tolstoy, is "the slave of history."

Determinism takes many forms. Marxism is the determinism of class. Nazism the determinism of race. But the idea of men and women as the slaves of history runs athwart the deepest human instincts. Rigid determinism abolishes the idea of human freedom—

the assumption of free choice that underlies every move we make, every word we speak, every thought we think. It abolishes the idea of human responsibility, since it is manifestly unfair to reward or punish people for actions that are by definition beyond their control. No one can live consistently by any deterministic creed. The Marxist states prove this themselves by their extreme susceptibility to the cult of leadership.

More than that, history refutes the idea that individuals make no difference. In December 1931 a British politician crossing Park Avenue in New York City between 76th and 77th Streets around 10:30 P.M. looked in the wrong direction and was knocked down by an automobile—a moment, he later recalled, of a man aghast, a world aglare: "I do not understand why I was not broken like an eggshell or squashed like a gooseberry." Fourteen months later an American politician, sitting in an open car in Miami, Florida, was fired on by an assassin; the man beside him was hit. Those who believe that individuals make no difference to history might well ponder whether the next two decades would have been the same had Mario Constasino's car killed Winston Churchill in 1931 and Giuseppe Zangara's bullet killed Franklin Roosevelt in 1933. Suppose, in addition, that Adolf Hitler had been killed in the street fighting during the Munich *Putsch* of 1923 and that Lenin had died of typhus during World War I. What would the 20th century be like now?

For better or for worse, individuals do make a difference. "The notion that a people can run itself and its affairs anonymously," wrote the philosopher William James, "is now well known to be the silliest of absurdities. Mankind does nothing save through initiatives on the part of inventors, great or small, and imitation by the rest of us—these are the sole factors in human progress. Individuals of genius show the way, and set the patterns, which common people then adopt and follow."

Leadership, James suggests, means leadership in thought as well as in action. In the long run, leaders in thought may well make the greater difference to the world. But, as Woodrow Wilson once said, "Those only are leaders of men, in the general eye, who lead in action. . . . It is at their hands that new thought gets its translation into the crude language of deeds." Leaders in thought often invent in solitude and obscurity, leaving to later generations the tasks of imitation. Leaders in action—the leaders portrayed in this series—have to be effective in their own time.

And they cannot be effective by themselves. They must act in response to the rhythms of their age. Their genius must be adapted, in a phrase of William James's, "to the receptivities of the moment." Leaders are useless without followers. "There goes the mob," said the French politician hearing a clamor in the streets. "I am their leader. I must follow them." Great leaders turn the inchoate emotions of the mob to purposes of their own. They seize on the opportunities of their time, the hopes, fears, frustrations, crises, potentialities. They succeed when events have prepared the way for them, when the community is awaiting to be aroused, when they can provide the clarifying and organizing ideas. Leadership ignites the circuit between the individual and the mass and thereby alters history.

It may alter history for better or for worse. Leaders have been responsible for the most extravagant follies and most monstrous crimes that have beset suffering humanity. They have also been vital in such gains as humanity has made in individual freedom, religious and racial tolerance, social justice and respect for human rights.

There is no sure way to tell in advance who is going to lead for good and who for evil. But a glance at the gallery of men and women in *World Leaders—Past and Present* suggests some useful tests.

One test is this: do leaders lead by force or by persuasion? By command or by consent? Through most of history leadership was exercised by the divine right of authority. The duty of followers was to defer and to obey. "Theirs not to reason why,/ Theirs but to do and die." On occasion, as with the so-called "enlightened despots" of the 18th century in Europe, absolutist leadership was animated by humane purposes. More often, absolutism nourished the passion for domination, land, gold and conquest and resulted in tyranny.

The great revolution of modern times has been the revolution of equality. The idea that all people should be equal in their legal condition has undermined the old structure of authority, hierarchy and deference. The revolution of equality has had two contrary effects on the nature of leadership. For equality, as Alexis de Tocqueville pointed out in his great study *Democracy in America*, might mean equality in servitude as well as equality in freedom.

"I know of only two methods of establishing equality in the political world," Tocqueville wrote. "Rights must be given to every citizen, or none at all to anyone . . . save one, who is the master of all." There was no middle ground "between the sovereignty of all and the absolute power of one man." In his astonishing prediction of 20th-century totalitarian dictatorship, Tocqueville explained how the revolution of equality could lead to the *"Führerprinzip"* and more terrible absolutism than the world had ever known.

But when rights are given to every citizen and the sovereignty of all is established, the problem of leadership takes a new form, becomes more exacting than ever before. It is easy to issue commands and enforce them by the rope and the stake, the concentration camp and the *gulag.* It is much harder to use argument and achievement to overcome opposition and win consent. The Founding Fathers of the United States understood the difficulty. They believed that history had given them the opportunity to decide, as Alexander Hamilton wrote in the first Federalist Paper, whether men are indeed capable of basing government on "reflection and choice, or whether they are forever destined to depend . . . on accident and force."

Government by reflection and choice called for a new style of leadership and a new quality of followership. It required leaders to be responsive to popular concerns, and it required followers to be active and informed participants in the process. Democracy does not eliminate emotion from politics; sometimes it fosters demagoguery; but it is confident that, as the greatest of democratic leaders put it, you cannot fool all of the people all of the time. It measures leadership by results and retires those who overreach or falter or fail.

It is true that in the long run despots are measured by results too. But they can postpone the day of judgment, sometimes indefinitely, and in the meantime they can do infinite harm. It is also true that democracy is no guarantee of virtue and intelligence in government, for the voice of the people is not necessarily the voice of God. But democracy, by assuring the right of opposition, offers built-in resistance to the evils inherent in absolutism. As the theologian Reinhold Niebuhr summed it up, "Man's capacity for justice makes democracy possible, but man's inclination to injustice makes democracy necessary."

A second test for leadership is the end for which power is sought. When leaders have as their goal the supremacy of a master race or the promotion of totalitarian revolution or the acquisition and exploitation of colonies or the protection of greed and privilege or the preservation of personal power, it is likely that their leadership will do little to advance the cause of humanity. When their goal is the abolition of slavery, the liberation of women, the enlargement of opportunity for the poor and powerless, the extension of equal rights to racial minorities, the defense of the freedoms of expression and opposition, it is likely that their leadership will increase the sum of human liberty and welfare.

Leaders have done great harm to the world. They have also conferred great benefits. You will find both sorts in this series. Even "good" leaders must be regarded with a certain wariness. Leaders are not demigods; they put on their trousers one leg after another just like ordinary mortals. No leader is infallible, and every leader needs to be reminded of this at regular intervals. Irreverence irritates leaders but is their salvation. Unquestioning submission corrupts leaders and demands followers. Making a cult of a leader is always a mistake. Fortunately hero worship generates its own antidote. "Every hero," said Emerson, "becomes a bore at last."

The signal benefit the great leaders confer is to embolden the rest of us to live according to our own best selves, to be active, insistent, and resolute in affirming our own sense of things. For great leaders attest to the reality of human freedom against the supposed inevitabilities of history. And they attest to the wisdom and power that may lie within the most unlikely of us, which is why Abraham Lincoln remains the supreme example of great leadership. A great leader, said Emerson, exhibits new possibilities to all humanity. "We feed on genius. . . . Great men exist that there may be greater men."

Great leaders, in short, justify themselves by emancipating and empowering their followers. So humanity struggles to master its destiny, remembering with Alexis de Tocqueville: "It is true that around every man a fatal circle is traced beyond which he cannot pass; but within the wide verge of that circle he is powerful and free; as it is with man, so with communities."

1
A Chance to Rule

As dawn broke on March 15, 44 B.C., a man woke with a start, rose from his luxurious sofa, and walked quickly to an open window. From his stately villa, which sat perched atop a hill that was densely planted with date and citrus trees, the man could see the sprawling metropolis of Rome. The dilapidated tenements of the poor, where in years past angry riots had broken out protesting the inequities of the Roman economy, crowded both banks of the river that bisected the city. At the base of one of the city's many hills stretched the Forum, a collection of public buildings and open areas that served as the religious, economic, and political center of Rome — another area that in recent years had borne witness to violent struggles. On this day, known to all Romans as the Ides of March, turmoil seemed a thing of the past. The city was at peace — due in large measure to the efforts of the dictator Julius Caesar and his lieutenant, Marc Antony, the 38-year-old Roman statesman who now stood by the open window.

As he moved from his bedroom to an adjoining chamber, where some of his slaves would shave him, curl his hair, and anoint his body with sweet oil, Antony seemed to epitomize the glory of Rome. Born into the Roman aristocracy, Antony had initially gained access to the corridors of power through suc-

Marc Antony delivers a funeral oration for Julius Caesar, the Roman dictator who was murdered by disgruntled senators on March 15, 44 B.C. Brandishing Caesar's torn and bloodied robe, Antony incited the people to a fury against the assassins.

A Roman coin bearing Marc Antony's profile. By early 44 B.C., after rising through a series of administrative posts and establishing strong ties to Caesar, Antony had become the second most powerful man in Rome.

cess as a soldier. He had fought in campaigns of conquest in such faraway lands as Gaul, Syria, and Egypt, proving himself a masterful horseman and a strong, decisive leader. The riches he acquired during those campaigns enabled him to buy influence in the corrupt world of Roman politics and to assume the trappings of aristocratic preeminence. In addition to his villa — a massive stone building with a huge library, elegant baths, stunning marble statues, and well-manicured gardens — Antony owned several large agricultural properties that were manned by hundreds of slaves captured in foreign wars. He frequently hosted elaborate banquets, where the fare included such delicacies as nightingale tongue and mice cooked in honey, and where the voracious consumption of spirits often led to childish frivolity and uninhibited sexual intermingling. By all accounts, he was extremely handsome; he had a graceful shock of curly hair, a rugged physique, and a boyish face. His looks, along with his legendary charm, won him the hand of a beautiful wife named Fulvia and the adoration of a sizable number of concubines.

But what made Marc Antony's life seem especially blessed was his close relationship with Julius Caesar, the master of Rome, a man who was revered as a symbol of authority and might. For many decades before the rise of Caesar, Rome had been governed by various competing factions of the noble class, who ruled the city through control of the Senate. As rivalries within the Senate became especially intense, Rome was plunged repeatedly into administrative stagnation, thereby leaving the government impotent to carry out much-needed reforms. In part out of a desire to remedy these ills and in part out of an unabashed thirst for power, Caesar — himself a member of the nobility — had in 49 B.C. declared war on the conservative faction of the Senate, which then controlled the state. He had gained sufficient power to do so after rising through a series of key government positions, conducting a successful eight-year military campaign against the nomadic tribes of Gaul (present-day France), and gaining the support of the common people — largely through ad-

Julius Caesar became dictator of Rome in 45 B.C. after
defeating the conservative faction of the Senate in the
Roman Civil War. During this conflict, Antony gradually
became Caesar's closest adviser.

A view of the Forum, the center of commercial, religious, and political life in ancient Rome. Around the central open area, where columns and statues commemorate the city's victories in foreign wars, are the Senate house, the hall of records, and several temples honoring the city's gods.

ept use of propaganda. During the four-year civil war, Caesar chased the senatorial army, led by Gnaeus Pompey (Pompey the Great), back and forth across the Mediterranean, to Greece, Spain, Egypt, and North Africa. After finally emerging the victor, Caesar had returned to Rome and seized autocratic control, receiving a succession of increasingly impressive titles: dictator, dictator for 10 years, dictator for life. He consolidated his rule by installing loyal politicians in all major offices and obtaining final veto power over all legislation (though as a magnanimous conqueror he did pardon many of the conservative senators and allowed them to return to Rome). At the same time, he had implemented an impressive array of reforms. He revamped Rome's debt-ridden financial system, corrected the calendar (which had become wildly out of step with the seasons), created economic opportunities abroad for the city's unemployed and devised an ingenious system for organizing the provinces.

Antony had played an integral role in Caesar's success. First linking up with Caesar in 54 B.C. as a commander in the conquest of Gaul, Antony was soon thereafter sent as the general's envoy to Rome, where he fought attempts by conservative senators to dismantle Caesar's army. During the civil war, Antony helped to lead Caesar's legions to victory over Pompey at Pharsalus, in Greece. Then, while Caesar took on senatorial forces in other locales, Antony returned to Italy and secured Caesar's control over the government of Rome. When Caesar finally took charge permanently, Antony became his closest adviser.

By March 15, 44 B.C., Antony was widely recognized as the second most important man in Rome. Still, on this morning he had woken up feeling uneasy. A few days earlier, a soothsayer had approached Caesar in the Forum and warned him to "Beware the Ides of March." On the succeeding night, all the windows in Caesar's house had blown open, and the dictator's wife had dreamed that he had been violently murdered. Although Antony was not usually superstitious, he had difficulty ignoring these portents. Having come to maturity in an era when Roman politics was dominated by intrigue, Antony was accustomed to regarding as valid even the most unlikely warnings of danger. Although the omens seemed to apply to Caesar, Antony knew that any threat to the dictator was likely to threaten him.

Adding to Antony's fear was his knowledge that there were men in Rome who disliked Caesar. A few sincere Romans were known to oppose his rule out of ideological opposition to the idea of dictatorship. Others, even some of Caesar's former supporters, were concerned less about his dictatorship than the extent to which he had extended its powers. His decisions were always automatically binding, and he had appropriated most of the elective offices for himself. Officials occupying the few positions he had not appropriated were required to swear not to overturn his laws. Many Romans were taken aback by Caesar's frequent abandonment of time-honored protocol, most notably his refusal to stand up from

> *When he was commander you had been his quaestor, when he was dictator, his master-of-horse, the chief mover of the war, the instigator of cruelty, the partner in his plunder.*
> —CICERO
> Roman statesman, on Antony's relationship with Caesar

his chair while conducting meetings of the Senate. But what truly had alienated Caesar's opponents was his adoption of the trappings of the monarchy that Romans had so painstakingly overthrown centuries earlier. He insisted upon sitting on a throne and always wearing triumphal dress. He ordered temples to be built in his honor, statues to be erected, and coins to be minted. He even went so far as to urge his followers to worship him as a god.

Shaken by these thoughts, Antony put on his white toga and leather sandals and prepared to go to the Senate, where Caesar would hold his last meeting before departing for a military campaign in the east. At the door he was greeted by the retinue of slaves, secretaries, assistants, and other hangers-on who accompanied him wherever he went. As he took a short walk in the garden before heading down the hill to the Forum, an assistant handed out bribes to those followers who had recently voted for one of Antony's measures or endorsed one of his candidates. Then it was time to go.

Slaves unload a small boat along the banks of the Tiber River in Rome. During Antony's day, goods were ferried to the capital in such vessels from the main Roman port of Ostia, which lay 15 miles down river.

Roman senators Marcus Brutus and Gaius Cassius watch as Caesar leads his entourage through the streets of Rome in 44 B.C. Although as dictator Caesar won the support of the people by enacting reforms, he alienated many senators with his arrogation of absolute power.

The cobblestone road down the hill to the center of the city was narrow and full of sharp turns. As Antony and his followers reached the commercial district, they felt the pace of the day quicken. Merchants busily set up wooden stalls to sell their wares. A salty breeze off the wharf bore the smells of sun-warmed pines, of baked breads, and grilling sausages. Antony's procession competed for room on the dusty lanes with ox carts carrying produce and meats from farms outside the city. On side streets, shutters snapped open, women set up their laundry lines, and children played ball games. The natural rhythms of a typical day in Rome temporarily allayed Antony's concerns about his political future.

But soon thereafter he reached the entrance to Pompey's Theater, where the Senate had convened ever since their regular meeting hall burned down. A large crowd had gathered outside to await the approach of Caesar. When the dictator arrived on a litter carried by his servants, the crowd swarmed around him, some kissing his hand, others seeking his attention on political matters; one man pushed through the crush of people and handed Caesar a note, but in the excitement of the moment, Caesar did not bother to read the message. Instead, he walked confidently into the theater. Meanwhile, Antony was drawn into conversation outside the building with a senator named Gaius Trebonius.

The members of the Senate rose as the ruler entered the hall. Several lawmakers gathered about Caesar, including Tillius Cimber who stepped forward and requested his assistance in securing the recall of his exiled brother. When Caesar attempted to push by the petitioner, Cimber caught hold of his toga and pulled it from his shoulder. This apparently was the signal.

A senator named Casca moved up behind Caesar, pulled a long dagger from his toga, and cut a shallow gash in the ruler's throat. The dictator was temporarily stunned and slightly injured, but he reacted, as usual, with lightning speed, turning around to confront his assailant and stabbing the man in the arm with a metal pen. As Casca withdrew, Caesar discovered to his horror that several other men had also drawn knives and had surrounded him. One by one the men stepped forward and plunged their daggers into the disbelieving ruler's body. Finally overwhelmed by the onslaught, Caesar fell in a heap, drenching the floor with his blood. He had received 23 wounds in all, the last inflicted by a man named Marcus Junius Brutus, a man who had opposed Caesar during the civil war but who had since become one of his closest friends. As Caesar lay dying — ironically next to the base of a statue of Pompey, his former rival — he uttered a final cry: *"Et tu Brute"* (And you too Brutus).

Caesar's supporters in the Senate remained frozen where they stood, afraid to interfere lest they too become victims of the assault. Antony, who had attempted to gain entrance to the hall after the attack began, had been detained by Trebonius. In all, the conspiracy had involved more than 60 senators. It had been masterminded by Brutus and Gaius

Fearing that Caesar sought to become king, more than 60 senators took part in his assassination, depicted here in an 18th-century engraving. As Caesar was stabbed to death at the base of a statue of Gnaeus Pompey, Antony futilely tried to intervene.

Though he was a close friend of Caesar, Marcus Brutus (depicted here in a bust by Michelangelo) joined the assassination plot in an attempt to restore the Roman republic. After the murder the assassins lost the support of many commoners.

Cassius. As Antony had guessed it might, the conspiracy had come from those who had the greatest reason to dislike Caesar — those who had lost to him in the civil war. Antony was not on friendly terms with this group. When the murder was done, the entire Senate fled Pompey's Theater. Antony, who had reason to worry that Caesar's assailants might come for him next, borrowed the clothes of a commoner and headed toward his villa in disguise. Arriving home, he ordered his slaves to put up barricades and took a moment to consider his situation.

His first reactions were grief and shock. He had served as Caesar's lieutenant for almost 10 years and had developed enormous respect for him. Frequently he had declaimed that Caesar had "inbred goodness." At the same time, he was also immensely disappointed. Caesar had taken power by force, and there was no established pattern for his succession. So now after working for so many years to secure a position of prominence in Rome, Antony faced the possibility of losing all his power to the conspirators or to some other faction of the Senate.

But in a certain sense, Antony welcomed the death of Caesar. Though always a loyal servant, he had begun to resent Caesar's unwillingness to treat him as a peer and had come to dislike the dictator's inability to convey warmth on a personal level. As Antony calmed down, he began to realize the tremendous opportunity that lay open to him: this could be his chance to become leader of Rome. Of course there were enormous obstacles to be overcome. He would have to secure the loyalty of Caesar's political backers, gain control over the deposed ruler's financial and military resources, establish dominance over the Senate, and outbid Brutus and his men for the loyalty of the people. At the same time, he would probably need to establish relations with the conspirators — at least in the short run — to guarantee his safety. Nevertheless, Antony had a chance to become ruler.

As Antony considered his options, the assassins were marching to the Capitoline Hill to celebrate what they termed Rome's "new liberty." Many of the commoners, unsure whom to follow, accompanied the conspirators. After dedicating their weapons, the assassins named Marcus Cicero as their candidate for new ruler of Rome. Cicero had not participated in the conspiracy, but among those who favored a return to a republican form of government, he was the most respected politician in Rome; he had held Rome's highest elective office, *consul*, in 63 B.C. Cicero was the greatest speaker and writer of his day, but when he did not appear at the gathering, the responsibility was left to Brutus to address the crowd. Brutus's speech showed that the conspirators had no long-range strategy for governing, aside from a vague desire to restore the republic. Roman citizens, yearning for a quick return to order, were repelled by this display of disorganization. Having enjoyed under Caesar, however briefly, the benefits of reform, the people were especially disturbed by the suggestion that the corrupt and self-interested aristocracy would reassume control. At the conclusion of the ceremony, as the popular reaction became clear, the assassins withdrew into the Capitol building and fortified themselves against attack.

Receiving word of these events, Antony felt secure enough about his immediate safety to begin his quest for power. It was a situation perfectly tailored to his greatest strength: the ability to act cooly and decisively under pressure. His first move on the afternoon of March 15 was to seek the backing of Caesar's army, led by Marcus Aemilius Lepidus. (At that time, there was no official Roman army; instead, armies were raised and funded by individual generals.) In a city where political struggles often escalated into armed conflict, military support was essential. Antony caught up with Lepidus in a field called the *Campus Martius*, where the general had ordered his troops in preparation for an assault on the conspirators, who were themselves defended by only a few gladiators. Realizing that Lepidus himself might pose a threat, Antony offered him the position of *pontifex maximus*, or chief priest, one of several administrative posts opened up by Caesar's death. The position was supposed to be elective, but Antony quickly dispatched an aide to pay the necessary bribes to make the appointment official. Lepidus, who had been a die-hard follower of Caesar, immediately accepted Antony as his leader, as did his troops.

Continuing to move quickly, Antony met during the night with Caesar's widow, Calpurnia. He convinced her to hand over the dictator's state papers and his fortune (estimated at $30 million). The money would prove useful in paying the salaries of Caesar's army and buying the support of prominent politicians. Possession of the papers would lend an official air to Antony's claim to be Caesar's rightful heir.

On March 17, Antony convened the Senate, not at Pompey's Theater but at the Temple of Tellus, a building near his home where he felt safer than in the heart of the city. Although most of the senators had initially been given their seats in the parliamentary body by Caesar, now the majority of them seemed to favor the republican plan. As the meeting began, an attempt was made to discredit Antony by declaring as invalid all of Caesar's edicts and measures. But Antony cleverly headed off this proposal by pointing out that if it were to be implemented, several senators who had been given prestigious appointments by Caesar would lose their offices. The republicans backed down. With the withdrawal of the proposal, Antony shrewdly gained the Senate's de facto acknowledgment that Caesar's rule had been legitimate — thus discrediting the conspirators' major justification of their act. Antony then won many of the republican senators over to his side by defeating a proposal by Caesarian senators to punish the assassins. Similarly, Antony kept the republicans from granting honors to the plotters. By the end of the meeting, Antony had shown himself to be a voice of moderation and an adept parliamentary maneuverer. He was now recognized as the true leader of the Senate.

The next day, Antony negotiated peace between his followers and the conspirators. Offering his own son as a hostage, he convinced Cassius, Brutus, and the others to emerge from the Capitol building. With

Heavens! What a man and how great you would have been had you been able to keep your resolution of that day!
—CICERO
Roman statesman, on Antony's speech at the Temple of Tellus

the encouragement of the people, who had milled about the public centers of Rome in large crowds since the beginning of the crisis, representatives of the two factions shook hands. That night Antony invited Cassius to his villa for dinner, adding a personal touch to the rapprochement.

On March 18, a second meeting of the Senate gave Antony's faction a boost by agreeing to hold a state funeral for Caesar. Two days later — when Caesar's will was read — Antony received a temporary setback. He was shocked to learn that Caesar had designated his 18-year-old nephew and adopted son Octavian (Gaius Julius Caesar Octavianus) as heir. Because Antony's grab for power had so far been justified by his claim to be Caesar's heir, this news was quite damaging. Nevertheless, Antony was little concerned about the threat of Octavian, who was only a youth with little power to speak of.

The funeral was held on March 20 at the Forum. Caesar's body was placed on a ceremonial couch

A marble frieze from Antony's day portrays a procession of senators. After overcoming his grief at the death of Caesar and resolving to challenge the conspirators for control of Rome, Antony quickly established his dominance over the Senate.

that was inserted along with his bloody garments in a model of a temple the dictator had been constructing to honor Venus Genetrix, a goddess from whom he had claimed ancestry. Services began with actors playing scenes from Caesar's life and reciting verses about his murder at the hand of men whose lives he had once saved. Then Antony rose to deliver the eulogy. In a masterful piece of rhetoric, he avoided directly attacking the assassins, which would have jeopardized his relationship with republican senators, but still managed to inflame the common people against Brutus's men.

As William Shakespeare later rendered the event in his play *Julius Caesar*, Antony began by insisting that Brutus was an "honorable man," repeating the facetious statement at rhythmic intervals. He

In his will, Caesar named his grandnephew, Octavian, as heir to his fortune and political position. When the will was read, Antony's claim to be Caesar's successor was temporarily called into question.

also repeated several times Brutus's claim that Caesar was ambitious. But then he undermined both assertions with profuse illustrations of Caesar's self-less devotion to the common people — "when that the poor have cried, Caesar hath wept." Although insisting, in Shakespeare's words, that he had come "to bury Caesar, not to praise him," Antony did just the opposite, exhaustively chronicling Caesar's achievements. He also demonstrated ample evidence of his own feelings for the man. "My heart is in the coffin there with Caesar,/ And I must pause till it come back to me." Antony concluded his address by reading from official transcripts of Senate proceedings the oaths all senators had taken to protect Caesar from harm.

By the time he had finished, Antony had shown the assassins to be brutal and hypocritical and had reminded the people of the many things Caesar had done for them. He had worked the crowd into a fury. The mourners built a raging fire beneath the embalmed corpse and threw everything at hand onto the pyre. From the fire they took burning sticks and ran through the streets crying "kill the murderers." They were prevented from burning down the houses of the assassins only by the efforts of slaves and neighbors. Ultimately, Brutus, Cassius, and the others were forced to flee the city. With the elimination of the conspirators, Antony was now master of Rome. He had accomplished this feat by acting cooly and decisively under pressure. But many questions remained. Would he be able to develop a long-term strategy for remaining in power and remedying the problems of Rome? Would he be able to fend off the challenges to his authority by young Octavian and maintain the loyalty of the republican senators? Would he be able to avoid the tendency he had shown in the past to lapse into irresponsible and decadent behavior when no crisis was at hand? Antony's journey had truly just begun.

> *You, I say, kindled those torches, those alike by which he was half cremated, and those by which the house of Lucius Bellienus was set on fire and burnt down.*
> —CICERO
> Roman statesman, on the effect of Antony's funeral oration for Caesar

2

Young Aristocrat

The violent murder of Caesar was only one of several cataclysms that shook the foundations of Rome during the 1st century B.C. Even before Antony was born in 83 B.C., the city had seen tremendous social upheaval and political conflict. Rivalry between various factions of Rome's ruling class had on three occasions led to civil war. Several of Rome's foreign provinces, poorly governed, and often exploited, had rebelled against Roman rule. And, in 90-98 B.C., inhabitants of the Italian peninsula outside Rome proper had become fed up with their lack of full Roman citizenship and had initiated the Social War. Much of this turmoil could be traced to the stresses and strains of Rome's expansion from a small, agriculturally oriented city-state with rustic traditions to a vast empire that included parts of Europe, the Middle East, and Africa. Growth had brought changes in social composition, an upheaval in values, and the onset of corruption in government, changes to which Rome's institutions, developed during its early years, had difficulty adjusting.

Rome was founded by the twins Romulus and Remus in 753 B.C. At the outset, it was a tiny city, inhabited by farmers and shepherds and ruled by a series of kings from a tribe to the north called the Etruscans. In 509 B.C., a small group of upper-class families known as *patricians* expelled the last king

> *The bankrupted aristocrats were as ready as the hopeless masses to follow the ambitious general to a political revolution.*
> —ELEANOR G. HUZAR
> American historian

According to legend, the twins Romulus and Remus were fathered by Mars, the god of war, but were abandoned as babies and raised by a she-wolf. In 753 B.C., the brothers united several tribes of farmers and herdsmen to form the city of Rome.

and established a republic. At first, this elite group maintained tight control over the new state's semi-democratic institutions and elective offices, to the exclusion of the lower classes, or *plebeians*. Executive power in the government belonged to two consuls, who were elected to one-year terms; they were supplemented by many levels of administrators and by the Senate, whose members, though officially delegated only an advisory role, wielded significant power as a result of owning lifelong appointments. Unity between patrician families was maintained by their organization into a small number of clans that were linked together by marriage alliances. Relationships between patricians and members of the lower classes were governed by the ancient custom of *clientship*, whereby each patrician was responsible for safeguarding the military, legal, and economic interests of several plebeians or "clients." He did so in exchange for control of his clients' votes in the assembly of all citizens, the *Comitia Curiata*. Although there was some resentment among the lower classes toward this system, the republic remained stable in its early years. This was due in part to the patricians' skill as rulers; in part to the republic's small size, which enabled the system of clientship to bind all citizens in a tight, cohesive unit; and in part to Rome's relative isolation, which helped to preserve ancient religious and social customs.

Over the following two centuries, however, Rome fought a series of wars that helped to make the political system more democratic. During the 5th century B.C., the city launched campaigns almost every summer against hill tribes to the north, and during the 4th century, it successfully repelled several invasions by nomadic Celtic-speaking tribes called the Gauls. By 275 B.C., Rome had expanded its territory to include all of the Italian peninsula south of the Po Valley. But because Rome had no standing army, the city's politicians were forced before each campaign to raise new battalions, in most cases drawing heavily upon plebeians who were forced to serve without pay as an obligation of citizenship. Gradually the lower classes came to resent the injustice

> *The relationship was a sacred bond whereby the patron offered military, legal, and economic protections in return for loyal services, including the clients' vote when a member of the patron's family stood for election.*
>
> —ELEANOR G. HUZAR
> American historian,
> on the clientship system

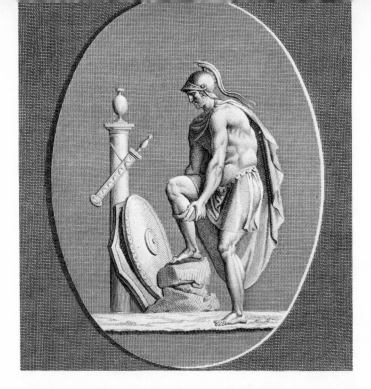

An idealized rendering of a Roman soldier equipped in a fashion typical of the early republic. After the republic's foundation in 509 B.C., upper-class leaders launched a series of campaigns against Rome's neighbors to the north.

of having to serve as shock troops in wars in which they received none of the spoils, whereas at the same time being denied a voice in government. Their dissatisfaction grew as the campaigns became increasingly elaborate, leaving them with less and less time to earn their livelihoods. Eventually, they decided to focus their dissatisfaction on seeking democratic reform. Capitalizing on their indispensability to Roman military goals, by 287 B.C. they had won significant concessions from the patricians.

They were granted the right to run for all political offices and were given 10 officials, *tribunes*, to safeguard their interests; elected to one-year terms, the tribunes had power to veto all laws passed by the Comitia Curiata and the Senate and all decisions made by the consuls and lower-level officials. The plebeians also forced the creation of a second assembly, the *Comitia Tributa*, over which they had control. The Comitia Tributa could pass binding legislation — laws called *plebescites* — without Senate approval, and it was charged with electing all of Rome's lower officials: the tribunes, the *aediles* (supervisors of public markets and roads), and the *quaestors* (financial officials and aids to provincial governors). Those plebeians who were elected con-

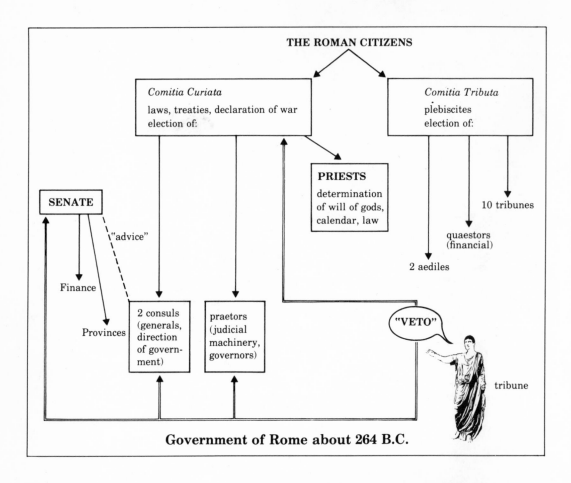

THE ROMAN CITIZENS

Comitia Curiata
laws, treaties, declaration of war
election of:

Comitia Tributa
plebiscites
election of:

PRIESTS
determination
of will of gods,
calendar, law

SENATE

"advice"

Finance

Provinces

2 consuls
(generals,
direction
of govern-
ment)

praetors
(judicial
machinery,
governors)

10 tribunes

quaestors
(financial)

2 aediles

"VETO"

tribune

Government of Rome about 264 B.C.

By 264 B.C. Rome's lower classes had forced the upper classes to allow them equal representation in government, through the mechanisms shown in this diagram. However, a new elite nobility came to dominate this seemingly democratic system.

suls, or *praetors* (state judges), attained status as patricians and earned lifetime memberships in the Senate. The patricians did maintain their domination of the Comitia Curiata, which elected consuls, praetors, and priests. Nevertheless, Rome seemed in 287 B.C. to be on the verge of becoming a democracy.

But continued growth of Rome's empire fundamentally altered the structure of society, undermined ancient customs, and led ultimately to the decay of democratic process — although democratic institutions officially remained in place. By the time Antony was born, Rome had become master of the Mediterranean, controlling an empire that extended beyond the Italian peninsula to include Cisalpine Gaul (present day northern Italy), Sicily, Sardinia,

Corsica, Narbonese Gaul (southern France), Illyricum (west coast of Yugoslavia), Africa (Tunisia), Asia (western Turkey), Achaia and Macedonia (southern and northern Greece), and Cilicia (southeastern Turkey). The provinces were connected to Rome in various ways. Those that came under Rome's influence during the early days of expansion were regarded as allies and were required, in order to demonstrate loyalty, to provide troops to Rome's wars. Those that had joined the empire later had been conquered in brutal wars and were forced to pay severe annual taxes in the form of currency or grain. The sprawling empire was knit together by an elaborate system of roadways and a standardized legal code. On the whole, however, Rome maintained a rather loose grip on its domains. The cen-

The Roman empire in 100 B.C., 17 years before Antony's birth. Rome had acquired its provinces through political alliances and military conquests. They were administered by governors who tended to ignore their duties in favor of enlarging their personal fortunes.

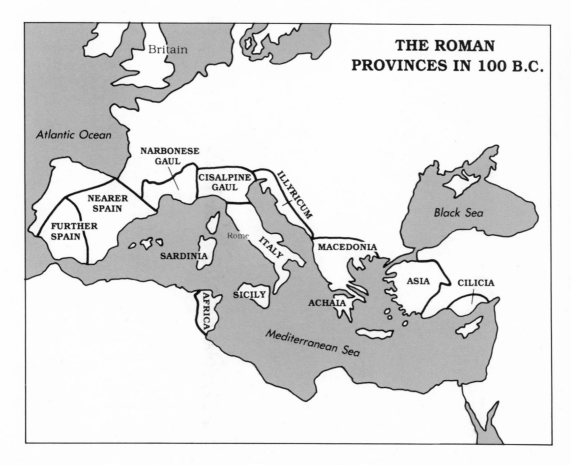

THE ROMAN
PROVINCES IN 100 B.C.

Britain

Atlantic Ocean

NARBONESE
GAUL

CISALPINE
GAUL

ILLYRICUM

NEARER
SPAIN

FURTHER
SPAIN

Rome

ITALY

SARDINIA

MACEDONIA

Black Sea

ASIA

CILICIA

AFRICA

SICILY

ACHAIA

Mediterranean Sea

tral government interfered sparingly in the activities of provincial governors, who maintained small staffs and spent little of their time on matters of regional administration, concentrating instead on expanding their fortunes by soliciting gifts and conquering outlying regions.

Provinces provided wealth to the city in many other ways. During the initial conquest of provinces reluctant to join the empire, Roman generals and their troops traditionally seized huge stores of jewels, currency, clothing, armor, grain, and pottery. Once under Roman control, provinces served as important sources of raw materials and as valuable markets for manufactured goods.

The massive infusion of wealth had profound effects on Rome, both positive and negative. On the one hand, taxes from the provinces enabled Rome to undertake an extensive program of public building. On the other hand, because money that accrued to private citizens was hoarded by generals, governors, and the business class, the gap was widened between Rome's rich and poor. As the city constantly grew in size, the ranks of the destitute swelled. Thousands of peasants fled to Rome from rural parts of Italy where they had been displaced by the giant slave-manned plantations of Rome's rich families. Rome also teemed with unemployed soldiers and foreign residents. To feed the masses, the government accumulated stores of grain in the warehouses of a giant structure called the Emporium, but delivery was often interrupted and prices were often too high. The horrible conditions in which the poor lived often produced health crises and violence.

Rome's new wealth and its inequitable distribution contributed to the spread of corruption in government. Romans with money gradually realized that they could buy political support with bribes, especially among the city's many impoverished citizens. Gradually, a new political elite called the nobles emerged, composed of rich families — patrician and plebeian — who could afford to spend enormous sums on bribery and political favors. The noble class was able to subvert the ostensibly democratic sys-

The clashes were obviously political in context and meaning. Disorder arose from political demonstrations, not as a feature of popular unrest.
—ELEANOR G. HUZAR
American historian, on
Roman political unrest

tem through bribery, extortion, and control of the Senate and thus determine the outcome of all magisterial elections and legislative votes. The nobles were linked together by marriage alliances and supported by vast networks of less-powerful Romans.

During the early years of the nobility's domination, there were no clearly discernible parties or factions. Though members of the Senate grouped and regrouped in constantly shifting bands, and though there was often intense competition between these various bands during elections, the Senate, whenever faced with a challenge to its authority from other parts of society, always united to preserve its oligarchic hold on power. But toward the end of the 2nd century B.C., members of the Senate gradually became divided into two camps, the *populares* and the *optimates*. This split fueled political conflict and hampered efforts to bring about social reforms or to amend political structures to accommodate internal changes. Although they never coalesced into actual political parties, the two factions were sharply distinguished by the contrasting manner in which they sought the passage of legislation. Populares tended to ignore the time-honored custom of introducing laws only in the Senate and pursued the more radical approach of appealing to the assembly of the people. They hoped eventually to bring

Rome's foreign wars brought tremendous riches to the city and supplied thousands of slaves to markets such as this one. But expansion also caused problems within the republic, widening the gap between rich and poor, undermining values, and fostering corruption in government.

A modern view of the Roman Forum, with the Capitoline Hill visible in the distance. During the 2nd century B.C., the Forum was the site of violent struggles between the two factions of the Roman nobility—the populares, who appealed to the people in seeking passage of bills, and the optimates, who upheld the supremacy of the Senate.

about permanent changes in the political system that would allow the votes of the people to carry greater weight. The more altruistic members of the populare faction favored such changes out of a genuine desire to make the system more democratic and to make it flexible enough to enact reforms; other populares sought the changes simply in order to advance their own careers. For their part, the optimates (also known as conservatives) viewed the authority of the Senate as inviolable. To their minds, every bill, every appointment, every election was the exclusive domain of the Senate.

Both factions were dominated by military generals, called "great men," who periodically took control of the government, taking advantage of the fact that Roman armies showed greater allegiance to their leaders than to the state. The first great man was the populare general Gaius Marius who ruled Rome during the first decade of the 1st century B.C. after crushing a rebellion in Africa and serving as consul from 104–100 B.C. In 90 B.C., when Marius saw his power threatened by the rise of Lucius Cornelius Sulla, an optimate general who attained special prominence with victories in the Social War, Marius had his rival's command revoked. In response, Sulla marched on Rome, beginning a civil war. Though Sulla won the first campaign in 89 B.C., Marius won the second in 88, and for the next five years the populares maintained their domination of Rome. Forced into exile during this period, Sulla conducted a campaign against Mithridates VI Eupator, of Pontus, who had started a rebellion in Rome's Asian province. But in 83 B.C., Sulla again marched on Rome. After winning the civil war of 83–82, he was named dictator and initiated a reign of terror in which thousands of populares were killed.

—Marc Antony was born in 83 B.C. into an aristocratic clan that had alternately been sympathetic to both major factions. He was the first of three sons born to Marcus and Julia Antonius. (To his contemporaries, Antony was, like his father, known as Marcus Antonius; it was only later, after he was immortalized in Shakespeare's *Julius Caesar* and *Antony and Cleopatra*, that historians began referring to him by the anglicized version of his name.) It was accepted as a foregone conclusion that Antony, like all male children of the nobility, would upon reaching manhood pursue a career in politics, attempting to advance up the ladder of administrative posts and elective offices known as the *cursus honorum* (racecourse of honors). In the rough-and-tumble world of Roman politics, he would have to develop a facility for political manipulation, accumulate vast stores of wealth with which to buy support, acquire a following of troops through military success, and endear himself to one or another of the great men. But like all aristocratic children, he would have an enormous head start: Upon reaching maturity he would inherit his family's large network of allies and supporters. In return he would be expected to deliver his vote to the faction with which his family had been recently voting.

From an early age, Antony was taught to respect his family's history. In the early years of Rome, the

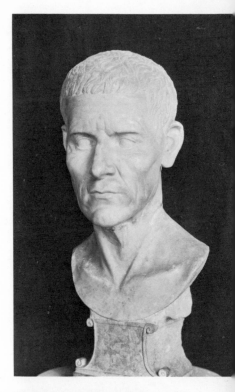

Lucius Cornelius Sulla was one of Rome's "great men," generals who dominated the Senate and who periodically took control of the state. In 82 B.C., Sulla, an optimate, defeated the followers of the populare leader Gaius Marius in a civil war and became dictator of Rome.

Antonius family had been low-ranking plebeians. After the plebeian class gained access to political office, however, several of Antony's forebears had served as consuls, which automatically gave the family patrician status. During the late republic, as many aristocratic clans became complacent and relied for position in society on the success of early ancestors, the position of the Antonii improved steadily.

The family attained special prominence during the career of Marc Antony's paternal grandfather, Marcus Antonius, who was born in 143 B.C. In his first years in politics, Antonius rose steadily through a series of elective offices, mostly by virtue of his speaking abilities. (Cicero would later pay homage to Antonius by making him the hero of a book entitled *The Making of an Orator.*) But in 112 B.C., while serving as a financial officer in the charge of the Asian governor, Antonius was almost ruined when he was implicated in a scandal. Although he could have avoided prosecution by remaining in Asia, he nobly returned to Rome and through a series of rousing speeches cleared his name. The episode ultimately provided a boost to his career. Later, after defending several conservatives in the Roman courts, Antonius was elevated to a leadership position in the optimate camp.

But it was through military success that Antonius truly became a major figure. In 102 B.C., as the official in charge of administering Roman ports along the coast of Cilicia, Antonius was assigned to conduct a campaign against pirates in the area. Given broad powers over all provincial governors in the region, Antonius spent the next two years recruiting an army, amassing a fleet, and finally winning several battles that not only reduced the influence of pirates in the region but also gave Rome enough control of the coast to establish a new province there. The Roman government rewarded him for his efforts by holding a celebratory parade in his honor, known as a *triumph*, and by erecting a statue of him in the Forum. His reputation as a military commander enabled him to achieve Rome's highest office, that of consul, in 99 B.C. As the Marian faction

Now mark the difference between you and your grandfather. He said deliberately what advanced his case: you at haphazard say what is irrelevant to it.

—CICERO
Roman statesman, on
Antony's political ineptness

A statue of a Roman orator. Antony's grandfather, Marcus Antonius, took advantage of exceptional speaking abilities to become, at the beginning of the 1st century B.C., one of Rome's most powerful men. Of his descendants, only Antony inherited his oratorical brilliance.

became ascendant in Rome, Antonius gradually changed his political sympathies, at first as a matter of expedience but later because he sincerely supported a program of reform. Also during the 90s, he followed Marius's liberal example in promoting full citizenship for Italian residents outside Rome proper. Sometime before 90 B.C., however, he fell out of favor with Marius after a personal conflict with one of Marius's closest aides. As a result, when Marius *proscribed* (designated for execution) thousands of his optimate opponents in 87 B.C., Antonius was put to death, and his head was nailed to the Rostra, the outdoor platform in the Forum from which major orations were delivered.

Though Antonius died an ignoble death, he was ultimately accorded a place of distinction in the minds of most Romans. His good name, along with

Early Romans worshiped 12 gods, whom they had appropriated from Greek mythology. One of them was Neptune (Poseidon to the Greeks), supreme god of the sea, who in the Roman pantheon replaced a simple water god who had protected farmers in early Rome from drought.

his enlargement of the family fortune and his expansion of its network of allies both at home and abroad, provided an enormous boost to the careers of his sons and grandsons, virtually guaranteeing that they would attain some sort of office. His descendants, including Antony, would be greatly influenced by his political views, tending to support reform legislation and to be sympathetic to Italian residents outside of Rome. But Antony would be the only one of his grandfather's descendants to inherit the qualities that made Antonius great — his oratorical brilliance, his skills as a military leader, and his ability to adjust to a constantly changing political climate.

For his part, Marcus, Antony's father, inherited little of his father's greatness. (For the sake of clarity, we will refer to Antony's grandfather as Antonius and his father as Marcus.) Though handsome and amiable and an extremely popular participant in the decadent world of Roman high society, Marcus proved ineffective in fulfilling the duties of the administrative posts his father's influence enabled him to acquire. Blessed with a large inheritance, he spent lavishly on generous gifts for friends and on clothes, slaves, and property for his family. He even went so far as to give away family silver to friends who were short of cash. Eventually, as was to be expected, he accumulated enormous debts, leading to frequent fights with his disapproving wife. It was said that Julia hired servants to spy on her husband's financial activities. Hence Antony's childhood proceeded against a background not only of political conflict but also of domestic turmoil and financial strain.

Nevertheless, Antony and his brothers received the same education that all aristocratic children were given to prepare them to join the elite. In accordance with Roman traditions, Antony's mother oversaw her son's development up to the age of seven. She hired a tutor to provide instruction in reading, writing, arithmetic, grammar, oratory, and literature. The purpose of Antony's education was to develop skills useful in a political career. Thus the tutor organized the curriculum to emphasize

> *Antonius's legacy to his son was, therefore, far from glorious: a fatherless home, a tarnished name, an overspent purse.*
> —ELEANOR G. HUZAR
> American historian

Mars was the most Roman of all the gods. His character changed with that of the Roman people; beginning as an agricultural deity for a farm-based society, he became the god of war as Rome became an aggressive and bellicose state.

analytical training and facility with language over math and science. During this period Antony "gave brilliant promise," according to Plutarch, a 1st-century Greek historian who included an account of Antony's life in his series of biographies called *Parallel Lives*. Nevertheless, Antony never showed any particular interest in academics and, unlike Caesar and Cicero, he would never be known for his intellectual prowess — although he would always be regarded as very intelligent. Julia herself took charge of Antony's moral and spiritual education, acquainting him with the traditional Roman virtues — endurance, frugality, simplicity, religious devotion, and upright dealing — necessary to become a *vir bonus*, a good man. Almost from the time he learned to speak, Antony was periodically hoisted on his mother's knee and told tales about early Roman heroes.

Most of Antony's lessons took place inside his parents' elegant house, which consisted of several spacious rooms that all opened onto a central courtyard, called an *atrium*. The central focus of the house was the hearth, where Antony was first exposed to Roman religious rituals. The Romans believed that human existence was controlled to a large extent by a family of gods, each of which was responsible for a different aspect of life. Romans attempted to please the gods and hence receive favorable treatment by making frequent animal sacrifices and conducting frequent ceremonies. Every day at dawn, Antony watched as his father threw a piece of salted cake onto the fire to honor Vesta, goddess of the hearth. Then the whole family participated in a second ceremony honoring the household gods, the *lares* (spirits of the ancestors) and the *penates* (guardians of the pantry).

Physical training was as important to a Roman boy's education as intellectual and spiritual development, and so with his younger brothers, Lucius and Gaius, Antony learned to swim, ride a horse, play ball, throw the discus and javelin, and box. Antony proved particularly adept at these activities, showing excellent coordination and remarkable strength. Exercise helped to develop Antony's rugged good looks. Even as a youth he displayed the physical traits that would later attract so many women to him — dark curly hair, broad forehead, determined chin, thick neck, and powerful body. He also began to show signs of what would later be his dominant personality traits. In the words of historian Eleanor Goltz Huzar, "His character was that of a battlefield warrior — for good and ill. Courageous, bold, loyal to friends, chivalrous to enemies, he was at his best when the challenge was the greatest and his slackest at times of ease."

When Antony was only nine, the order of his household was disturbed by his father's assignment to lead a major military expedition in the east against pirates who were disrupting Roman shipping in the Mediterranean. Marcus was the first Roman general ever to be given the *imperium infinitum*, which allowed him unfettered movement around the Mediterranean and unlimited time to

> *The old tales were retold, the old phrases reused, but the cohesive, consistent, committed spirit of early Rome was now a pose, not an actuality.*
> —ELEANOR G. HUZAR
> American historian

Venus, the Roman goddess of love, was originally only a goddess of horticulture who bestowed beauty and fruitfulness on gardens. Later her influence was extended, and she played a greater role in human lives.

complete his task. Ultimately, he used his expanded powers primarily to exploit Roman provinces. Under the pretense of gathering supplies for his mission, Marcus sailed to Sicily, Spain, and Byzantium, where he extorted large quantities of goods and money. As a pirate hunter, however, he was so completely inept that Roman coastal residents were said to fear his approach more than that of pirates. After trying for two years to engage the pirates in a major battle, he finally did so in 72 B.C. He was soundly thrashed and forced into a humiliating peace. In 71 B.C. he died in disgrace in Crete. He was later known to most Romans by the nickname "Creticus," in mocking reference to his inglorious demise.

The death of his father left Antony without a stable home life during his teens. Although Julia had been remarried to a man named Cornelius Lentelus, the man was weak and profligate and preoccupied with his political affairs. Aristocratic youths traditionally had devoted their teens to apprenticeships with Roman officials, but by Antony's day this custom had all but disappeared. As a consequence, many Roman youths sought stimulation by joining gangs that roamed the streets at night seeking idle pleasures and engaging in wild, often illegal behavior. Lacking any parental direction, Antony fell in with such a crowd.

Joining the gang of Publius Clodius, Antony spent his evenings frequenting the taverns along the municipal wharf, visiting brothels, lounging at the baths, flirting with slave girls in the market, gambling, and above all, drinking. Antony soon befriended a member of the gang named Gaius Scribonius Curio. With a similar fondness for frivolous merrymaking, the two became inseparable. In Curio's company, Antony greatly enlarged his debts, which had already become sizable from an effort to lay the groundwork for a political career. According to one historian, Antony's debts at this time totaled more than $300,000. For a while Curio helped Antony fend off the moneylenders by telling them that his father would cover the debts. But when Curio's father was forced to pay back a loan for Antony, he thereafter forbade his son to see the young wastrel.

As Antony grew to maturity, conflict in Roman politics between the populares and the optimates became increasingly intense. After the death of the dictator Sulla in 78 B.C., the two groups vied to fill the power vacuum, with the optimates gaining a slight advantage during the latter part of the 70s. But in the next decade, the populare leaders Gnaeus Pompey and Publius Licinius Crassus emerged as the preeminent figures in Rome, posing a major threat to the conservatives who were led by Marcus Porcius Cato and Marcus Cicero. Pompey won power through his success as a military leader, putting down a slave revolt led by Spartacus in 72 B.C., vanquishing several fleets of pirates in 67 B.C., and quashing Mithridates' second rebellion in Asia in 65 B.C. Crassus, who served with Pompey as consul in 70 B.C., made his name primarily through financial success, becoming one of the largest landowners in Rome by forming a private fire department, buying burning houses at ludicrously low prices, and then putting out the fires. During the mid-60s,

A fresco (wall painting) from the Roman city of Pompeii illustrates a typical ritualistic sacrifice. Pompeii, located near the modern day city of Naples, was buried beneath the ashes and lava of Mt. Vesuvius when the volcano erupted in 79 B.C. Excavated by modern archaeologists, the city is remarkably well preserved; its remains provide clues to how people lived during ancient times.

Crassus applied his enormous wealth toward advancing the career of his protégé, Julius Caesar, enabling the young man to buy the loyalty of thousands of Romans and to compete for government posts that had previously been beyond his reach. In 60 B.C. Crassus, Pompey, and Caesar formed a political alliance called the First Triumvirate. Blending Pompey's legendary military reputation and loyal political following with Caesar's own growing body of supporters and Crassus's huge fortune, the *triumvirs* were able to dominate Rome even though they were not officially Rome's rulers. The alliance catapulted Caesar to the consulship of 5 B.C., in which position he carried out reforms, sent Cicero into exile, reduced the influence of Cato by having him assigned as the governor of faraway Cyprus, and won a five-year assignment as governor of three provinces — Illyricum, Transalpine Gaul, and Cisalpine Gaul — from which he planned to stage campaigns of conquest in the untamed region of Gaul proper.

During this period, Antony took the first halting steps of his own political career. Despite his grandfather's ties to Sulla, Antony sided with the populares — with whom he would be connected for the rest of his life. At the outset, his radical sympathies were largely a product of his association with the gang of Publius Clodius. Although most of their parents were optimates, members of the gang came to support the populare program for change because of a natural rebelliousness, and because their status as major debtors put them at odds with the government in its existing form.

In 63 B.C. the gang was accused of having supported a plot by Catiline — the loser in that year's consular election — to overthrow the Roman state in a violent revolution. It was true that Clodius's bunch had tacitly endorsed the so-called Catilinarian Conspiracy — unlike the mainstream faction of the populares, who favored a moderate pursuit of reform. But the gang members had done so more out of a general antagonism to the status quo than out of an appreciation of the mercurial Catiline's half-baked scheme. In the end, even though Cicero man-

DISCOBOLO
DI MIRONE

The Discus Thrower, a famous Roman copy of a bronze statue by the Greek sculptor Myron. Antony's education included instruction not only in oratory, Roman history, and literature, but also swimming, boxing, and discus throwing.

aged to get the Senate to put those directly involved in the plot to death — after the ringleader himself disappeared from Rome — Antony and company were judged to have played an insignificant role and escaped prosecution.

In 62 B.C., Antony's crowd was discredited when its leader, Clodius, was put on trial for sneaking, disguised as a woman, into the house of his lover Pompeia, Caesar's wife, during the all-female religious rite celebrating *Bona Dea* (the "Good Goddess"). With the subsequent rise to power of the First Triumvirate, however, Clodius not only escaped prosecution but also became, as tribune for 59 B.C., a key member of the populare government. Antony himself served as Clodius's aide, helping to convince a Roman court to send Cicero into exile on charges of illegally gaining the execution of the Catilinarian conspirators.

By 58 B.C., the 25-year-old Antony had built several valuable alliances. Nevertheless, he realized that to compete for high office he would need additional training in oratory. So that year he left for Greece, where there were several exceptional speaking teachers. Historians have suggested that there were

A 19th-century French painting illustrates the schooling of Vestal Virgins, female children chosen from patrician families to serve as custodians of the temple of Vesta, the goddess of the hearth. Each morning during his childhood, Antony participated with his family in rituals honoring Vesta.

additional reasons for Antony's departure from Rome — that he may have grown tired of the decadent life-style of the Clodius group; that he may have sought to escape creditors; and that he may have gotten himself into hot water by having an affair with Clodius's wife, Fulvia. In any case, once in Greece, Antony devoted his full energies to becoming an adept practitioner of a flowery manner of speaking known as the Asiatic style. In addition to studying rhetoric, he frequently participated in military exercises conducted by local Roman armies. And it was as a soldier that Antony, with his great physical strength and natural ability to make quick decisions, stood out. In 57 B.C., Aulus Gabinius, a Roman general on his way to Syria to combat a rebellion, passed through the town in Greece where Antony lived. Witnessing Antony's expertise on the battlefield, Gabinius asked him to serve as his commander of cavalry. Antony considered it the offer of a lifetime.

A modern view of the Forum from the Capitoline, one of the seven hills of Rome. In 58 B.C., after establishing strong ties to the populare faction, Antony left Rome for Greece, where he planned to study public speaking.

3

Soldier

For Antony, the expedition to Syria with Gabinius's army was an opportunity to prove his worth as a soldier and to make valuable political connections. Gabinius was one of the most respected men in the populare faction, having served as Pompey's right-hand man for more than 10 years. In 67 B.C., as tribune, he had steered through legislation that granted Pompey his command to fight Mediterranean pirates, and while Pompey campaigned abroad, Gabinius had served as his envoy in Rome. With the ascension to power of the First Triumvirate, Gabinius's influence had increased proportionally, winning the election as consul in 58 B.C.

The campaign in Syria was considered crucial to the security of the Roman Empire. Syria was one of Rome's most valuable provinces, possessing enormous riches and serving as a barrier to incursions into the empire by the neighboring state of Parthia, Rome's aggressive rival in the Middle East. The province had lately been destabilized by a bitter dynastic struggle between two brothers in the Jewish region of Judea. In 63 B.C. Pompey, who was in the region to fight Parthia, had intervened in the conflict, helping Hyrcanus II to wrest control of the Judean throne from his brother Aristobulus II. After granting official Roman endorsement to Hyrcanus's regime, Pompey had taken Aristobulus and his family

His character was that of a battlefield warrior—for good and ill.
—ELEANOR G. HUZAR
American historian

In 57 B.C., at the age of 26, Antony joined the army of populare general Aulus Gabinius on an expedition to Syria, where a local dynastic struggle threatened the security of the Roman empire. Having impressed Gabinius at military exercises in Greece, Antony was named an officer in the cavalry.

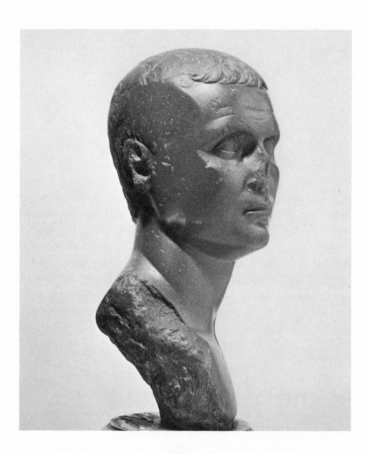

Blessed with great physical strength and a natural ability to act decisively in times of crises, Antony, in Gabinius's service, proved to be an excellent soldier.

back to Rome as prisoners. But in 59 B.C. Aristobulus's son, Alexander, had escaped from Rome and returned to Judea, where he routed Hyrcanus in battle, took control of Judea's major forts, and assumed the titles of king and Jewish high priest. Alexander's presence on the throne was considered a threat to Roman authority in the area, and Gabinius's mission was to overthrow him.

The general's army sailed across the Mediterranean from Greece in long, flat-hulled vessels called galleys, which were powered by oarsmen and durable leather sails. Upon reaching the coast of Syria, Antony and his fellow soldiers set out on an arduous march across the parched desert. Their destination was a walled city called Alexandrinum, one of Alexander's strongholds along the Jordan River northeast of Jerusalem.

Gabinius's army was an efficient fighting machine, composed of professional soldiers with many years of training and combat experience. Its main body was the infantry, which was divided into 5,500-man battalions called legions, each of which would be distinguished in battle by a separate standard. The infantry was supplemented by auxiliary units of scouts, cavalry, and archers, and a crew of engineers that was assigned to operate the army's sophisticated battle machines: earth-moving tools, battering rams, enormous catapults, and tunneling drills. Each soldier, including Antony, was armed with an iron-tipped javelin, a short stabbing sword attached at the belt, and a wooden shield covered with leather. Their uniforms consisted of plumed helmets with visors and tunics covered with iron *mail* (armor made of metal links).

In battle, Gabinius's army would depend on the quality that made all Roman armies of the era formidable: organization. Legions would be supervised by notoriously stern drill sergeants called *centu-*

A Roman officer's field armor. Each member of a Roman battalion, or legion, was equipped with an iron-tipped javelin, a short stabbing sword, a shield, and an ironmail tunic. Their distinctive plumed helmets bore the insignia of individual legions.

A bas-relief shows Roman soldiers overpowering their enemy. During Gabinius's year-long campaign in Syria, Antony played a key role in defeating the rebel Jewish king Aristobulus II and restoring Hyrcanus II to the Judean throne.

rions. As described by the Roman historian Polybius, centurions were "not so much bold and adventurous as men with a faculty for command, steady and rather of a deep-rooted spirit, not prone to attack or start battle, but men who in the face of superior numbers or overwhelming pressure, would endure and die in the defense of their posts." Coordination between and among legions would be facilitated by an intricate command structure. The deep loyalty each soldier felt for his legion would provide an additional cohesive force.

As Gabinius's well-equipped army moved in neat lines across the desert, they were an intimidating sight. When they reached the heart of Judea, they wasted no time in conducting an assault on the fortified city of Alexandrinum. Seeing his first combat, Antony at once proved his mettle, making his way over the high city walls before any of his compatriots. Once inside, he killed scores of rebels, fighting as if he really were — as he sometimes joked — descended from Hercules, a mythical Greek hero renowned for his strength. After the Roman victory, he was decorated heavily for his heroism and offered his first chance to lead men. His assignment was to take part of Gabinius's army on a foray against two forts in the Dead Sea area to which Alexander's men had withdrawn. Immediately showing a gift for leadership, Antony relentlessly laid siege to the strongholds, giving the rebels no choice but to sue for peace. The fighting resumed when Aristobulus slipped out of Rome and regrouped his son's army. In the climactic battle, Antony led a successful second assault on Alexandrinum that permanently ended the Judean revolt.

After the final victory, Gabinius and his men enjoyed the spoils of war, dividing up the fortune of the defeated branch of the family. Otherwise, however, Gabinius acted with restraint in reasserting Roman control over the region. Although he sent Aristobulus to Rome in chains, he spared the rest of the Judean king's family the harsh treatment that Rome's martial foes usually received. He ordered his men to keep a watchful eye on Roman tax collectors and moneylenders in the area to keep them from exploiting the Judean people, and he attempted to provide greater political stability to Judea by redistributing power from the central government to five regional councils directed by Jewish notables. Antony was deeply impressed by the Roman general's behavior. In later years, as a provincial governor, he would be influenced by Gabinius's example.

Although Gabinius treated the Judeans magnanimously, he still had plans to exploit the citizens of outlying regions in order to offset financial losses he had incurred in the consular election of 58 B.C. He planned to launch a quick strike against aggressive Arabs who had violated Syria's eastern border and to wage a major campaign against Parthia. But, as his army began its march toward these areas, Gabinius received word of events transpiring in Egypt that led him to scuttle his plans.

Egypt was an independent kingdom along the southern edge of the Mediterranean that had for centuries been a major center of trade and culture. Even before the foundation of Rome, Egypt had built

It was characteristic of Antony to show his finest qualities in the hour of trial, and indeed it was always when his fortunes were at their lowest that he came nearest to being a good man.
—PLUTARCH
Roman historian

Ptolemy I was the first in a long line of Macedonian kings to rule Egypt. His descendant Ptolemy XI (Auletes) was overthrown by the Egyptian people in 58 B.C. after failing to stave off Roman domination.

a flourishing economy by taking advantage of bounteous farmland enriched by the floodwaters of the Nile River. Its capital city, Alexandria, founded by the Macedonian conqueror Alexander the Great when he ruled the country for a short period, boasted the ancient world's finest architecture, best schools, and most innovative artists. The country had been ruled for almost 300 years by the Ptolemies, a line of kings descended from the Macedonian family to whom Alexander the Great had bequeathed the southern part of his empire. For several generations, the Ptolemies had ruled effectively and enjoyed popular support. But during the 1st century B.C., as the common people began to resent rule by foreign kings, Egypt suffered from growing internal disorder. At the same time, the Ptolemies faced the external threat of Roman invasion; Egypt was the only land along the Mediterranean that had not yet been taken by the empire.

For Ptolemy XII Auletes, who assumed the Egyptian throne in 80 B.C., staving off Roman domination became an obsession that ironically led him to cultivate closer ties with Rome's leaders. When Pompey's governorship of Syria in 63 B.C. brought him uncomfortably close to Egypt, Auletes sent him presents of money and military supplies in order to stay in his good graces. In 59 B.C., Auletes traveled to Rome in order to petition its rulers to grant official recognition of his right to the Egyptian throne. Faced initially with resistance from the triumvirs Crassus and Caesar, who wanted to annex Egypt, Auletes showered influential senators with generous gifts. Finally, Auletes managed to negotiate a deal with Caesar, who was in desperate need of funds to repay campaign debts and to mount an army for his upcoming expedition to Gaul. Borrowing a large sum from the Roman financier Rabirius Postumus, Auletes paid Caesar to force a resolution through the Senate recognizing Ptolemy as an "ally and friend of the Roman people."

Although Auletes had saved Egypt's independence — at least temporarily — he did not receive a hero's welcome upon returning to his country, for in the meantime Cyprus, Egypt's last overseas possession, had been taken over by Rome. Not wanting to disturb his precious alliance, Auletes did not register a protest against the Roman move, even though his brother, the ruler of Cyprus, had committed suicide during the attack. The Egyptian people were furious. Their anger increased when they learned that Auletes expected them to pay back his debt with Rabirius Postumus. In 58 B.C., the citizens of Alexandria staged an armed rebellion, driving Auletes into exile and catapulting his daughter, Berenice, to the throne.

In his attempt to regain control, Auletes again turned to his Roman benefactors. First appealing to Cato, the new Roman governor of Cyprus, he was told that his cause was futile: "All Egypt turned into gold would no longer satisfy the greed of the Roman politicians," Cato said. Not willing to concede defeat, Auletes traveled on to Rome, where with the help of Rabirius — who was concerned that without Roman support Auletes would have to default his loan — he managed to get a hearing before the Senate. But without the aid of Caesar, who was preoccupied with his campaigns in Gaul, Auletes had difficulty swaying the conservative faction of the Senate, which was then ascendant. Though willing to give moral support, the conservatives opposed providing troops to Auletes, fearing that the Roman general who received the command, with its promise of extraordinary prestige and riches, might become dangerously powerful.

In January 56 B.C. they tried to block action on the basis of religion, claiming to have found a passage in the Sibylline Books that warned against aid to Auletes. The books, a collection of prophetic writings kept at the temple of the oracle Sibyl, had purportedly counseled, "If the king of Egypt comes asking for help, do not refuse him friendship, but do not give this aid with a host [an army] or you will meet troubles and dangers." The conservatives had almost surely concocted the passage themselves, but the Roman people, who tended to be more religious and superstitious than their leaders, rallied behind the prophecy, and Auletes' cause was doomed.

As a last resort, Auletes appealed to Gabinius as a general with a large army in a state adjacent to Egypt. Although Gabinius was aware of the Senate's prohibition, he decided to help Auletes after being promised a staggering sum of gold. His decision was influenced by his realization that Syria's proximity to Egypt would enable him to accomplish the mission before Roman leaders could discover or protest it. Many of Gabinius's officers recommended against the campaign, but Antony supported it wholeheartedly, tantalized by rumors of Egypt's fabulous wealth, anxious to win further glory as a soldier, and aware that the triumvirs supported Auletes. As official justification for the expedition, Gabinius made the dubious claim that Egypt's new leader Berenice had been encouraging pirates on the North African coast and that she had ordered the construction of a massive fleet with which the country planned to challenge Rome.

In the fall of 56 B.C., the difficult campaign began. To get to Egypt, the army had to overcome immense hardship and constant privation. Trekking across the vast Sinai desert, they encountered harsh gusting sands and intense heat, losing scores of pack animals to dehydration. As they approached their destination, they were forced to wade through hip-deep, mosquito-infested swamps where the soupy air abounded with exotic diseases. Along the way, Antony greatly impressed his men with his willingness to share all dangers and difficulties. He inspired them with his high spirits, cheering them on when they slogged through the bogs. When the army finally reached the Egyptian border, they faced a further obstacle: To gain access to the country's interior they had to capture Berenice's stronghold at Pelusium, which lay at the far end of a treacherous isthmus. Antony and his cavalry were chosen to lead the way. After crossing the land bridge in the midst of intense enemy fire, Antony recruited the assistance of Jews living on the edge of Pelusium and took the city in a lightning assault. As he would do after most battles during his career, Antony extended clemency to the prisoners he had captured and prevented the spiteful Auletes, who followed the

[Alexandrians] liked him personally and used to say that Antony put on his tragic mask for the Romans but kept the comic one for them.
—PLUTARCH
Roman historian

cavalry into Pelusium with Gabinius, from carrying out executions.

The Roman army then advanced along the coast and through the Nile Delta to Alexandria, where Berenice's main army was stationed. The Egyptian army put up a valiant effort, but their cause was ruined when Antony's cavalry slipped around to the far side of the city, completing the Roman encirclement. After the Roman victory, Antony was awarded high honors. Restored to the throne, Auletes meted out harsh punishment to the vanquished, even executing his own daughter Berenice. By contrast, Antony was the paragon of generosity. One of the casualties in the fighting, Berenice's lover, Archelaus of Cappadocia, had befriended Antony during his time in Greece. Antony, after scouring the battlefield to find Archelaus's corpse, honored his friend with a ritual eulogy. This display of kindness won Antony the lasting respect of the Egyptian people, which would prove valuable during his later tenure as Roman ruler of the east. Gabinius's army stayed for a time in Alexandria, giving Antony the opportunity to appreciate the glories of the city — its white marble buildings, its magnificent works of art, its theaters, public libraries, and schools. He

A wall painting from an Egyptian tomb. Antony partook of the cultural riches of Alexandria, Egypt's capital, after participating in Gabinius's successful military campaign to reinstall Auletes as king. During his stay in Alexandria, Antony was introduced to Cleopatra.

also met Berenice's 14-year-old sister, Cleopatra, with whom he reportedly fell in love at first sight.

In Rome, the news of Gabinius's success in Egypt had not met with the excitement that he had anticipated, but had instead generated outrage. In 56 B.C. he requested a triumphal parade; instead he was censured by the people's assembly. In early 54 B.C., after he and Antony had defeated a huge Jewish army at Mount Tabor in Judea, Gabinius gave up his command and returned to Rome amid a firestorm of controversy. He immediately faced trial on two charges: Conservatives offended by his flouting of the senatorial decree on Egypt accused him of treason; tax collectors peeved by his interference in their activities in Syria accused him of extortion. Ultimately, he was fined more than he could pay and fled into exile. Although Antony had played a major role in Gabinius's victories, he escaped prosecution when the Senate decided that he had simply been following orders. Nevertheless, determining that it would be best to be out of Rome for a while, he headed toward Gaul, where a position in Caesar's army awaited him.

Coveted for many years by Roman imperialists,

A frieze adorning an ancient Roman sarcophagus, or stone coffin, illustrates a battle between Romans and Germans. From 54–53 B.C. Antony fought against the nomadic tribes of Gaul as a junior officer in Caesar's army.

Gaul was a vast independent land comprising much of modern-day France and inhabited by more than 200 nomadic tribes, most of which had migrated to the area 8 centuries earlier from the eastern side of the Rhine River. Though politically disorganized and disunited, the Gauls otherwise boasted an advanced civilization, having made significant strides in agriculture, metallurgy, pottery, and public speaking and having established a sophisticated network of trade along Gaul's many rivers. To Caesar, the largely uncharted region had seemed to present the perfect opportunity to enlarge his fortune and to win the favor of the Roman people. Taking advantage of his extraordinary governorship of the three neighboring Roman provinces, Caesar had campaigned in Gaul every summer since 58 B.C., returning each winter to the southern side of the Alps to be closer to political developments in Rome. For the most part acting without proper Senate approval, Caesar had fought a series of successful battles against Celtic, Belgic, and Germanic people, on a number of occasions killing off whole tribes in brutal massacres. By 56 B.C. he seemed to have established control of all of Gaul; news of his victories had earned him tremendous renown in Rome. In 55 B.C. he had won his first naval victory, made a brief trip to the exotic isle of Britain, and led Rome's first expedition to the far side of the Rhine River. As Antony reached Gaul in early 54, the general seemed to be at the height of his power. For Antony, a job with Caesar offered the chance to establish further connections in the populare camp and to learn about military strategy from a master.

The particulars of Antony's first year of service in Caesar's army are shrouded in mystery. Most of what is known about the wars in Gaul comes from Caesar's own book, the *Commentaries*, which, although it contains prose that is considered among the best in Latin, mentions nothing about junior officers like Antony. It is known that during this period Caesar undertook a second, more extensive expedition to Britain, throwing five legions at the combined British tribal armies and finally overwhelming their leader, Cassivelaunus, in a climactic

He went from Egypt to furthest Gaul before going home. But what home? For every man possessed his own home then, and nowhere was there one of yours.
—CICERO
Roman statesman, on Antony's wanderlust

battle at the capital city of Wheathampstead. And it is probable that Antony, as a cavalry officer, participated in the mission because Caesar had beforehand constructed specially designed vessels that enabled him to bring along his horsemen. Caesar's army also undertook a major campaign in 54 B.C. to restore order in Gaul, where there had been several tribal attacks on the forts he had set up to maintain his authority in the region. The battles in Gaul lasted well into autumn.

Antony must have served with at least some distinction in the two campaigns, for in the spring of 53 B.C., Caesar chose to make him a political protégé. As the first step in promoting Antony's career, Caesar sent him to Rome with sufficient funds and endorsements to run for his first public office. He was to vie for a position as one of Rome's 20 quaestors, financial officials who either worked for the state treasury or in the service of a provincial governor. If and when elected, Antony was expected to return to Gaul to work as quaestor under Caesar. Before the elections of 53 B.C. got under way, however, order in Rome was completely disrupted by a dramatic rise in political violence and an outbreak of riots. The operation of government gradually ground to a halt.

Tensions in Rome were exacerbated by the gradual dissolution of the First Triumvirate. In 54 B.C., Julia, Caesar's daughter and Pompey's wife, had died, destroying one of the major links between the triumvirs. Then, in early 53 B.C., Crassus was killed while conducting a campaign against Parthia in the east. Without the conciliatory force of the third triumvir to hold them together, Caesar and Pompey were transformed from friends to rivals, and their representatives initiated skirmishes against each other in the public areas of Rome. Ultimately, the elections were delayed for almost a year. Antony himself became involved in the violence as he waited. In the middle of a riot in the Forum, Antony got into an argument with his old friend Clodius and attempted unsuccessfully to stab the gangleader with a sword. Historians offer conflicting interpretations of Antony's motives for the attack;

some postulate that he was simply carrying out orders for Caesar, who had had a falling out with Clodius after their collaboration in 59 B.C., but others suggest that Antony's action grew out of a personal feud with Clodius, stemming from Antony's affair with his wife, Fulvia.

In early 52 B.C., the Senate finally became fed up with the violence in Rome and, abandoning standard procedure, appointed Pompey sole consul with wide powers to bring the chaos to a halt. Although the Senate's decision was a setback for Antony's political faction, it did lead in February 52 B.C. to the resumption of elections. Antony easily won the quaestorship in a campaign riddled with graft. Afterward he hurried off to Gaul where Caesar faced another crisis.

The Gallic tribes, for so long divided by territorial rivalries and administrative weakness, had finally become united around a mutual hatred of Caesar. Under the strong leadership of Vercingetorix, a brash and confident young nobleman, the disparate tribes had merged their armies and in the winter of 53–52 B.C. had launched a full-scale revolt against Roman rule. Caesar had rushed to the scene, leaving his headquarters in Cisalpine Gaul much earlier than usual; by summertime, after several fierce battles, he had managed to trap Vercingetorix and his army of 80,000 warriors inside the walled city of Alesia (just north of Dijon), where he hoped to starve the Gauls out. It was at this time that Antony reached Caesar's army.

Soon after Antony's arrival, Gallic leaders in other regions recruited 250,000 fresh troops and led them to the aid of their besieged comrades. After failing in an attempt to break through the outside of the Roman lines, the Gallic reinforcements implemented their own siege, surrounding the Romans. To protect his troops from the Gallic siege, Caesar ordered his engineers to construct a ring of trenches and fortifications 14 miles in circumference around the outside of his camp, similar to the 11-mile double wall that already protected the inside. For their part, the Gauls inside Alesia were protected by massive walls and by the natural barrier of rugged terrain. There was only one side of Alesia not fronted by hills, and it was on this three-mile plain that Antony was assigned by Caesar to command several Roman legions.

Gradually, as the Romans relentlessly held their ground, the Gauls trapped inside Alesia began to run out of supplies. Finally, Vercingetorix resolved to throw all of his resource into a final all-out attack. In the first eight-hour encounter of the battle, neither side made any headway. The Gauls began the second with a midnight attack on both the interior and exterior Roman walls. Antony's men had difficulty holding their positions and required help from other battalions; the Romans were saved only by their artillery and the ingenious device of digging holes in the earth and hiding stakes in them. At noon the next day, the third and final part of the

Vercingetorix, a charismatic Gallic nobleman, united the disparate tribes of Gaul in 52 B.C. and mounted a fierce rebellion against Roman rule. After losing to Caesar in the climactic battle of Alesia, he rode into the Roman camp, surrendered, and laid down his weapons before the Roman general.

battle began. Sixty thousand Gauls streamed out of Alesia and mobbed the Romans' hillside positions. Riding back and forth along the Roman lines, Caesar and Antony worked in tandem to ensure that fresh troops manned each area. Though the Romans were woefully outnumbered, the sight of their leaders braving enemy fire inspired them to reverse the tide of the battle and to force the Gauls on the outside ring to retreat. Ultimately, a distraught Vercingetorix rode down from Alesia on his horse, laid his weapons at Caesar's feet, and surrendered. The Gallic leader was later carted back to Rome in chains, to be paraded as proof of Caesar's success.

For his important role in the defeat of Vercingetorix, Antony received extensive honors. While Caesar completed his conquest of Gaul by defeating a series of minor rebellions, Antony rose to become his second-in-command, often taking charge of the main army while Caesar ventured off on mop-up operations. By the end of 51 B.C., Antony's quaestorship had expired. He had proved himself to be an outstanding soldier and a brilliant commander. He had made invaluable connections with Caesar's foreign allies. He had become a rich man through captured loot and a large salary from Caesar. And, most important, he had gained Caesar's trust. Now, for great general and dependable lieutenant alike, it was time to return to politics.

4
Caesar's Henchman

Antony traveled to Rome in early 50 B.C., hoping to continue his advance up the political ladder and to create favorable conditions for Caesar's return. For Roman provincial governors like Caesar, the transition to civilian life was always difficult, for upon giving up their commands they automatically forfeited their immunity to prosecution. As a result, they inevitably faced trials on charges of extortion, bribery, brutality, using force in politics, and other crimes committed as a matter of course by men in their position. With the optimate bloc in power behind the leadership of Pompey, the transition promised to be especially treacherous for Caesar. During his first years in Gaul, Caesar had anticipated this problem and forced through a law that entitled him to remain in Gaul while running *in absentia* for the consulship in 49 B.C., a position whose term overlapped with his governorship and that also conferred immunity. With the optimates in power, however, there was the constant danger that the law would be overturned.

With orders from Caesar to safeguard this law and to rally support for the populares among the people, Antony announced his candidacy in 50 B.C. for the political office of tribune and the religious office known as *augur*. The position of augur was a lifetime post whose holder was responsible for reading

Julius Caesar completed his conquest of Gaul in 51 B.C. and prepared to rejoin Roman politics. Because the government was then dominated by the rival camp, the optimates, Caesar could not return to Rome immediately and instead dispatched Antony as his envoy.

religious omens to determine the wishes of the gods. In Rome's early years the post had normally been filled by members of a priestly class who sincerely believed in religion, but by Antony's day it had become the exclusive province of atheistic nobles, who exploited its far-reaching powers for political ends. If elected as augur, Antony would be allowed to use omens as justification for sending enemies into exile, overturning laws, pardoning criminals, and dissolving legislatures. The position of tribune entitled its holder to veto all government measures and appointments.

During the campaign, Antony did everything he could to woo the commoners, whose votes, as registered in the Comitia Tributa, would determine both elections. He used Caesar's money to buy generous gifts for the poor, held elaborate parties to solidify ties with Caesar's network of clients, and made promises that, if elected, he would seek to lower the price of grain and to redistribute public land. He was assisted by the efforts of the incumbent tribune, his old friend Curio, who on the day of the election worked the people into such a fury that

The Persian sun god, Mithras, whom the Romans adopted during the 1st century B.C., sacrifices a bull. In 50 B.C. Antony was elected augur, or omen interpreter, a position that was commonly exploited for political gains.

there were riots in the streets in favor of Antony. Caesar himself sent a battalion of soldiers to swell the ranks of the populare faction. Ultimately, Antony won both positions by huge majorities. Hearing the news in Gaul, Caesar was especially pleased by Antony's selection to succeed Curio as tribune. Because Caesar drew most of his support from the people and had few powerful allies in the upper echelons of the nobility, he needed constant access to the tribunician veto to check his conservative opponents.

Antony was to take office in December. In the meantime, as tribune-elect, he fought vigorously in the Senate against conservative attempts to strip Caesar of his immunity by dissolving his command in Gaul prior to the consular election of 49 B.C. Pompey and the conservatives feared that if Caesar were allowed to return to Rome, he would be able to use the riches and military power he had acquired in Gaul to take control of the state. On several occasions, the tribune Curio, with Antony's endorsement, vetoed laws that would have nullified Caesar's command. Eventually, this led to governmental stalemate.

On December 1, Curio and Antony attempted to break the impasse by offering a clever compromise. They proposed that Caesar would give up his army in Gaul on the condition that Pompey forfeit his own command in Spain. A huge majority — 370 out of 392 senators — voted to approve the measure, reasoning that without some sort of compromise the conflict between Pompey and Caesar would soon escalate into an unwanted civil war. But conservative leaders obtained a veto. Having heard false rumors that Caesar had begun an invasion of Italy, the conservatives took the additional step of asking Pompey to raise troops to defend the state. Conservative consul Marcus Marcellus made the request personally, going to Pompey's headquarters outside the city and placing a sword in his hand. Curio vetoed Pompey's commission, but the veto was ignored. Caesar himself, discovering that he had lost his one tool for checking the conservatives, the tribunician veto, began mobilizing troops. It seemed that war was at hand.

Caesar crosses the Rubicon River in 49 B.C., starting the Roman Civil War. Antony had unsuccessfully attempted to forestall such a conflict by negotiating with Caesar's rival, Gnaeus Pompey.

But at the behest of Senate members who were alarmed by Pompey's mobilization, negotiations continued throughout December. After taking over as tribune on December 10, Antony served as Caesar's primary agent during these negotiations. He made various proposals, even suggesting at one point that Caesar would be satisfied with the allotment of a single legion and the governorship of the relatively insignificant province of Illyricum, but Pompey would not yield. Even as the governor of Illyricum, Pompey reasoned, Caesar would pose a threat. On January 1, 49 B.C., at a Senate meeting, Antony tried to read a letter from Caesar reiterating his refusal to give up his command unless Pompey followed suit. He was shouted down. The Senate

Gnaeus Pompey joined Caesar and Publius Crassus in 60 B.C. in the First Triumvirate, a political alliance that for many years dominated Rome. The alliance dissolved after the death of Crassus in 53 B.C.

proceeded to pass a measure demanding that Caesar relinquish his command by a certain date or be declared an outlaw, and on January 7 they officially validated Pompey's de facto dictatorship and instituted martial law. Antony finally had to dress up as a servant and sneak out of town in disguise to avoid being murdered.

Waiting with his troops in Cisalpine Gaul, Caesar decided to give up on negotiations. Declaring "the die is cast," he led his men across the Rubicon River, which separated Cisalpine Gaul from Italy. In so doing, he committed treason, violating Sulla's law prohibiting a provincial governor from commanding troops outside his dominion. It was an irreversible step. The conflict known to history as the Roman Civil War had begun.

Although Pompey had the support of the government and, theoretically, all the provinces, Caesar was confident of victory. He quickly moved down the Italian coast, welcomed triumphantly in all towns he passed through. Antony joined him on the way and immediately assumed control over part of the army. Within a month, Pompey had been driven to the foot of the Italian peninsula, where his army

An 18th-century French painting shows Hercules, a mythic Greek hero known for his strength, being transformed from a human being into a god. Antony, said to bear a physical resemblance to Hercules, claimed to be the Roman incarnation of the Greek figure.

Roman soldiers on the march, as represented in an engraving based on a frieze that decorates Trajan's Column
in the Forum. In 48 B.C. Caesar caught up with Pompey's
army at Pharsalus, Greece, and, with Antony serving as
second-in-command, defeated his former ally.

boarded galleys and fled to Greece. While Caesar took on Pompey's forces in Spain, Antony ruled Rome as his representative. In January 48 B.C., Caesar sailed to Greece in pursuit of Pompey. Finally catching up with him in August, their armies met at the Battle of Pharsalus.

During the battle, Caesar put Antony in charge of the army's left wing. There his vigorous attack broke the enemy line and sent Pompey's army fleeing, ending the first part of the civil war between Pompey and Caesar and securing Caesar's power in Rome. Caesar named Antony Master of the Horse, next in power to himself, and left him in charge of Italy while he went to defeat Pompey's forces in Africa.

During this lull Marc Antony grew bored. With no battles to fight and nothing to engage his vast ener-

A relief from the base of a marble column illustrates a charge by Roman cavalry and foot soldiers. From 48 to 45 B.C., after the assassination of Pompey in Egypt, Caesar fought two more campaigns against his followers in Africa and Spain.

A portrait of Caesar by the early Renaissance master Mantegna. After the civil war ended, Caesar returned to Rome and was given a series of successively higher titles — dictator, dictator for 10 years, dictator for life. Antony encouraged Caesar's imperial ambition.

gies, he fell back into the bad habits of his youth: He drank and caroused and spent money. He incurred enormous debts, buying presents for his many lovers and funding extravagant banquets and picnics. He used up lovers as swiftly as he had mowed down enemies; he drank too much and vomited in public, and in general he made a sad spectacle of himself.

When Julius Caesar returned to Rome in 46 B.C., Antony's carousing stopped at once. At Caesar's firm suggestion, Antony paid bills he had been ignoring and in general began to curb his profligate behavior. Later, though, the sadder side of his personality would lead him into real trouble. For Antony would not have Caesar to rule over him very much longer, and with Caesar's death he would begin learning his life's hardest lesson: that the gods chose men not only for triumph but also for tragedy.

5

Triumvir

After routing the conspirators who had assassinated Caesar, Antony sought to increase his power further by taking over the governorship of Cisalpine Gaul. Although the position officially belonged to Decimus Junius Brutus (not related to Marcus Brutus), one of the assassins, Antony used his mastery of the Senate to have it transferred to him. In October 44 B.C., after Brutus indicated that he would not relinquish control of the province, Antony assembled an army and headed northward to seize it by force.

During Antony's absence, Caesar's intended heir, Octavian, came to Rome to claim his inheritance. Octavian had little experience in politics, but he quickly gained the support of many senators who had lost faith in Antony after determining that he sought simply to become another dictator like Caesar. Many welcomed the sickly 18-year-old Octavian, thinking that he could be used and later discarded. Cicero, in particular, championed Octavian, savaging Antony in a series of harsh speeches known as the *Philippics*. Ultimately, Cicero convinced the Senate to declare Antony an enemy of the state and to throw its full support behind Octavian, who also had won the loyalty of Caesar's army.

The result was another civil war. Octavian was authorized to lead troops against Antony for the purpose of securing Brutus's command in Cisalpine Gaul. In 43 B.C., Antony was defeated at Modena and forced to flee across the Alps. While Antony re-

The program of the triumvirs was to defeat the republican assassins of Caesar and "to restore the republic." Their real goal was to rule the state unchallenged.
—ELEANOR G. HUZAR
American historian, on
Roman political alliances

Marc Antony feasting with Cleopatra, from a 16th-century mural by Veronese. Three years of violent struggle for control of Roman politics were abandoned in the winter of 40 B.C., when Antony fell prey to the charms of Egypt's seductive queen.

Octavian, Caesar's official heir, appeared at first to be an insignificant rival for Antony's power, having few political connections. But he managed to win the support of the Senate after Antony alienated the lawmakers.

grouped in Gaul, receiving reinforcements led by Lepidus, Octavian grew disenchanted with the Senate. Although Octavian was young, he was not naive; he knew the senators were only using him. In August 43 B.C., after the Senate refused to grant him a consulship, he assembled an army and invaded Rome. When he heard the news that Antony had established alliances with Lepidus and generals of other western provinces, Octavian decided to join forces with them. In November 43 B.C., Octavian, Lepidus, and Antony met at Bononia and agreed to form the Second Triumvirate. Unlike the First Triumvirate, the second became the official ruling body of Rome. Its powers were recognized by the Roman government in a law called the *Lex Titia*. It divided the primary Roman provinces among the three — Gaul to Antony; Spain to Lepidus; Africa, Sardinia, and Sicily to Octavian — and gave the triumvirs wide-ranging powers. Antony now had considerable security, because the only men powerful enough to oppose him were his corulers. But for this he paid an awful price: Earlier in his career he had been able to afford mercy, but now only ruthlessness would serve.

As a condition of the agreement, not only Antony's own political enemies but those of the other two rulers were killed and their property confiscated. Lists — known as *proscriptions* — of enemies of the state were posted on wooden tablets in the Forum. Many of Antony's close friends and relatives died in the Second Triumvirate's reign of terror. Antony was particularly brutal in his treatment of Cicero, demanding that upon Cicero's capture the head and hand of his longtime rival be cut off and displayed in the Forum. By the end of 43 B.C., Antony was indeed where he wanted to be — at the top — but the climb had been a brutal one, and to reach the summit he had had to agree to share power.

In 42 B.C., Antony and his fellow triumvirs turned their attention to eliminating the threat posed by the conspirators, who remained in exile. Led by Cassius and Brutus, the assassins had assembled a large army and had recruited Pompey the Younger, son of Pompey the Great and commander of the largest naval fleet in existence at that time. In the summer of 42 B.C., the enemies assembled opposite one another at the plain of Philippi in the land of Macedonia, north of Greece. By October their armies — a hundred thousand on each side — were at war. Brutus fought Octavian on the north, and beat him, but Antony's army to the south crushed Cassius. A few days later, when Brutus's army went down before the Triumvirate's combined forces, Brutus committed suicide. Antony covered Brutus's body with his own scarlet cloak and paid for his enemy's funeral.

From Philippi, Antony went to Greece to raise money for his army and to observe the activities of provincial officials and tax collectors. But lacking an immediate crisis, Antony again fell into old patterns of wanton behavior. When he entered a district, the people would dress up and throw enormous banquets for him; kings and queens vied for his favor while actors, dancers, musicians, and comedians filled his retinue. In songs they called him Bacchus the joyful and gentle, after the Greek god of wine (also known as Dionysus). Bacchus was also known to be savage and cruel, and Antony gradually began to live up to that side of his divine nickname as well.

In Asia Minor (where Antony travelled after leaving Greece), for example, he was approached by a group of flatterers who asked him to grant them the unclaimed estates of citizens they insisted were dead. Though Antony knew that the owners of the estates in question were still alive, he granted the request anyway, thus depriving innocent citizens of their houses. Although it did not topple empires, this kind of carelessness nevertheless injured people; meanwhile Antony went on having a good time. He had nearly superhuman energy during the times of crisis — during battles, while seizing power. But it seems he lacked a talent for long-range planning. He went triumphantly from challenge to challenge, but greatness is not fashioned only from individual triumphs. To endure, those triumphs must be fastened together by the cement of lasting purpose.

In Asia Minor in 41 B.C., Antony met Cleopatra. He immediately fell under the spell of her consid-

Cicero, the greatest orator and writer of his day, convinced the Senate to back Octavian in a war against Antony. After Octavian and Antony reconciled their disagreements and decided, with Lepidus, to rule Rome jointly as the Second Triumvirate, they conducted a reign of terror in which thousands of Romans, including Cicero, were put to death.

This panel by the 19th-century French master Jacques-Louis David depicts the dead sons of Marcus Brutus being brought home to their family, victims of the Second Triumvirate's proscriptions.

erable powers. In slyness and subtlety, in ambition, intelligence, and charisma, the 29-year-old Egyptian queen equaled any ruler of her time. Antony had summoned her to his camp at Tarsus to answer charges that she had provided aid to Brutus and Cassius in the battles at Philippi. She was glad to hear from him, for she had long been preparing a strategy for guaranteeing that Egypt would not fall under Roman domination. The strategy required as a prerequisite the cooperation of a powerful Roman like Marc Antony.

Cleopatra floated to Antony's riverside camp on a golden barge with purple sails. Perfumed slaves pulling silver oars propelled the barge, their strokes beating time to the music of harps and flutes. Maids dressed like sea nymphs worked the rudder, while boys in cupid costumes fanned the queen, who lay, dressed like Venus, beneath a gold awning. Later, when Antony had come aboard to have supper with her, Cleopatra gave a signal, and suddenly in the dusk thousands of tiny candles glued to branches were lit, so that the entire floating palace and the river took on the appearance of some magical forest.

It was an impressive show. As the candles flickered, Cleopatra worked her wiles on Antony. She was not beautiful in an ordinary way, but she had a more useful quality: she was charming. She could speak delicately or tell coarse jokes, depending on what was appropriate for the occasion. She was intelligent, but more, she knew how to make others feel intelligent. Her charm had worked on Julius Caesar, Pompey's son, and now Antony. In fact, it may have worked too well — for by the end of his first evening with her, Marc Antony was more than charmed: he was in love.

Antony had been married several times. In his youth, he wed Fadia, of whom we know nothing except that she was rich and bore him several children. Next he married Antonia, whom he divorced after becoming suspicious that she had committed adultery; after that came a long liaison with Cythera, an actress whom he did not marry. Finally he married Fulvia, who was his wife at the time he met Cleopatra.

In 42 B.C., the triumvirs finally eliminated the threat of Brutus and Cassius, defeating the conspirators at the two battles of Philippi. Afterward, a distraught Brutus fell on his sword, declaring, in Shakespeare's rendering of the event, "I shall have glory by this losing day/more than Octavius and Marc Antony/I kill'd not thee with half so good a will."

A bust of the Egyptian queen Cleopatra by an unknown Greek artist. In 41 B.C. Antony summoned Cleopatra to Tarsus, in Asia Minor, to explain her support for Brutus and Cassius. Beguiled by Cleopatra's charms, Antony fell in love with her.

But no woman could hope to compete against Cleopatra. She was rich and lovely, smart and funny, haughty and tender. After their memorable first meeting in Tarsus, Antony decided to spend the winter of 41–40 B.C. in Egypt with her. At her side in Alexandria, Antony spent the next few months in glorious celebration. Together they gave dinners, went hunting, played games, drank, and rambled through the streets at night singing. When they were together, they were always laughing. Cleopatra amused Antony with her follies, flattered him, and made love with him, so that for months on end he was happy.

Antony's wife Fulvia, however, was furious. As a way of forcing Antony to leave Cleopatra to come back to Rome, she joined with Antony's brother Lucius in declaring war against Octavian in the spring of 40 B.C. Meanwhile Parthia, Rome's constant enemy to the east, was raiding Roman territories in Asia. Both circumstances required Antony's immediate attention. He was forced to leave Egypt, not to see Cleopatra again for three years. But he would not forget her.

Antony spent the winter of 40 B.C. with Cleopatra in
Egypt, which for centuries had been a center of culture
and trade in the Mediterranean world. Egypt's wealth
stemmed primarily from its bounteous farmland, enriched every year by the flooding of the Nile River, as
depicted in this Roman mosaic.

6

Reconciliation and Defeat

In the spring of 40 B.C., Antony hastened to Rome. By the time he got there, Fulvia had been soundly defeated by Octavian in the Battle of Perusia and had died in the process. Octavian held Antony responsible for Fulvia's actions and, upon Antony's return to Rome, prepared to renew the war against his fellow triumvir. But he was restrained from doing so by his army, which threatened to mutiny if the fighting continued. Rome had enough problems, they argued, without having to endure yet another civil war. Taxes were skyrocketing, unemployment was soaring, food was scarce. Ultimately, the triumvirs agreed to a reconciliation, which was sealed by the Treaty of Brundisium in 40 B.C. In addition to reaffirming the Second Triumvirate, the treaty redistributed power in the alliance, greatly reducing Lepidus's share of the empire and significantly enlarging Antony's and Octavian's. While Lepidus received only the small province of Africa, Antony gained control over the entire eastern half of the empire and Octavian assumed leadership of the provinces in western Europe.

To further affirm their renewed friendship, the two ascendant triumvirs agreed that Antony would marry Octavian's favorite sister, Octavia. Although he loved Cleopatra, Antony accepted the nuptial ar-

It was hoped that if only Octavia . . . could become united to Antony and win his love . . . this alliance would prove the salvation of their own affairs and would restore harmony to the Roman world.
—PLUTARCH
Roman historian, on Antony's marriage to Octavian's sister

A bust of a Roman soldier. Antony had to leave Egypt in the spring of 40 B.C. after his wife, Fulvia, declared war on Octavian. The short conflict briefly threatened the Second Triumvirate, but the triumvirs reaffirmed their ties later that year in the Treaty of Brundisium.

rangement, understanding its political import. It would, Antony reasoned, make Octavian less likely to attempt to seize solitary control of Rome. It would also help to allay the fears of the Roman citizenry that Antony's affair with Cleopatra might lead him to move the capital of the empire from Rome to Alexandria.

With his position in Rome secure, Antony turned his attention to Parthia, which had continued to make incursions into the province of Syria during the year 40 B.C. From 39 to 37 B.C., Antony's army carried out the campaign against the aggressive kingdom on its own; while he lived in Greece, spending much of his time making merry. Increasingly he encouraged his attendants and provincial subjects to view him as the incarnation of the Greek god Bacchus, the god of wine. On several occasions, he was celebrated in Dionysian (or Bacchanalian) rites, evening-long orgies of drinking and carousing that involved long frolics through wooded terrain and sometimes resulted in violence. In 37 B.C., the year in which the triumvirate was due to expire, Antony temporarily halted his binging in order to travel to Italy, where he and Octavian extended the alliance another five years. The peace was called the Treaty of Tarentum. Also, in that year, Antony received a shipment of supplies from Cleopatra that he intended to use in his upcoming battles with Parthia. In exchange for the provisions, Antony ceded his lover two pieces of his eastern domain — Phoenicia and northern Judea. He also secretly agreed to marry her at some unappointed date, in order to make legitimate their two children, the twins Helios and Cleopatra Selene.

In 36 B.C., Antony finally undertook the campaign he had been planning for so many years. Parthia promised to be a formidable foe. In June 36 B.C., the Parthians had inflicted on Crassus the worst defeat Rome had ever suffered, killing the distinguished general and three quarters of his men. The Parthians had surprised Crassus's men with an unusual military tactic: Riding on camels, the Asian archers had fired a steady stream of arrows at two different trajectories, rendering Roman shields use-

> *Antony's finest qualities as a man and as a soldier were evident in this crisis, and only his leadership kept the retreat from becoming a rout.*
> —ELEANOR G. HUZAR
> American historian, on the Parthian crisis

less. It was said that when Crassus's head had been delivered to the Parthian king on a platter, the king ordered molten gold to be poured into the rich man's mouth, saying, "Here, you have been greedy for this all your life. Eat it now."

In the last three years, Antony's lieutenant, Ventidius, had won several battles against the kingdom; now Antony meant to finish the job. From the beginning, however, Antony's campaign was handicapped by his preoccupation with Cleopatra. Having amassed a huge war treasury and a force of more than 100,000 men, Antony had acquired a significant edge over his enemy, but he squandered this advantage in his haste to return to Cleopatra's side. Antony's army had to complete a difficult march across Asia Minor to get to Parthia, and Antony should have stopped in Armenia at the end of the trek so that his men could rest and prepare. Instead, he charged impatiently forward toward Phraata, one of the principal enemy cities. Along the way, he ordered his army to abandon much of its heavy machinery, insisting that it slowed them down. Three hundred wagonloads of siege equipment were left behind, along with an eighty-foot battering ram — all of which would eventually be appropriated by Parthia. When Antony's troops reached Phraata, they immediately began an assault. But having jettisoned the tools with which they normally built siege mounds, they had enormous difficulty getting over the Parthian city's high walls. As a consequence, they were badly defeated. The Roman death toll was 10,000 men.

As Antony regrouped his army outside Phraata and considered his next move, he suffered an additional setback. In recruiting allies for his mission, Antony had gained the services of the Armenian king Artavasdes, whose nation had on several occasions been invaded by Parthia. But now Artavasdes withdrew his support, convinced by the Romans' ineptitude in the initial battle that defeat was inevitable. Meanwhile, inside the walls of Phraata, the Parthians threatened counterattack.

For Antony, to find himself in danger of losing to Parthia must have been a sobering experience. In

A bronze statue of Isis, the powerful goddess of Egypt's harvests whom Cleopatra claimed as her own divine mother. Cleopatra encouraged Antony to claim a similar divine heritage.

A stone relief of Cleopatra in the Egyptian traditional style, wearing the serpent crown of the Nile. Cleopatra contributed substantially to Antony's campaign against Parthia, begun in 36 B.C. Antony, in his haste to return to the queen, rushed too quickly into the campaign, with disastrous results.

part his failure had stemmed from his preoccupation with Cleopatra, but it also was related to his arrogance. At one time, Antony had been content with his role as a mere assistant to Caesar. Now he insisted that his followers revere him as a god — as a descendant of Hercules, or Bacchus. Cleopatra, who often fancied herself to be the incarnation of Isis (the Egyptian goddess of fertility), encouraged him in this tendency. His arrogance had been fanned by the ease with which he had risen to power. In almost every venture that he had undertaken, he had succeeded. So as he plunged overzealously into the Parthian fiasco, he had come to imagine that he could never lose.

After that stunning initial defeat, however, Antony exhibited a different trait: the ability to thrive in time of crisis. Just when it seemed that he would go down in defeat, he conceived a new plan. He ordered his troops to break camp as though they were

The Greek inscription on this stele describes Cleopatra's ritual offering to Isis. The child in her lap may represent Caesarion, her son by Julius Caesar.

Roman soldiers in hand-to-hand combat. Antony's troops were at a disadvantage against the Parthians, having been ordered to abandon most of their siege equipment before reaching the Middle Eastern kingdom. Antony's enormous tactical error cost the Romans many thousands of lives in the end.

heading back to Rome; then, after marching for a day, he had them wheel around and launch a surprise attack on the Parthians, who had followed them across the desert. Although most of the enemy troops escaped back to Phraata, the Romans had clearly shown themselves to be the superior army. After the battle, Antony asserted his authority over his troops by meting out harsh punishment to a group who had contemplated desertion — executing one man for every ten in the group.

With the Romans and the Parthians each having won one battle, the situation reached a temporary

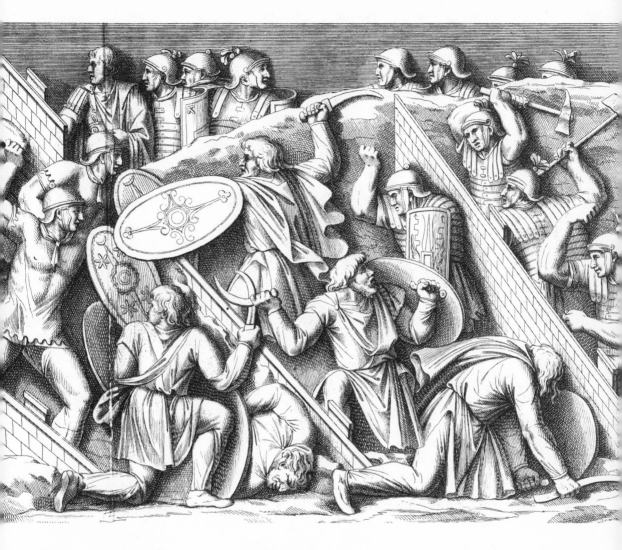

stalemate. Behind the impenetrable walls of their fortress, the Parthians were temporarily safe from harm, while the Romans, for their part, had set up a fierce blockade outside the city. But each side knew that something had to give before winter. If the stalemate continued beyond that time, the Parthians would start running out of food, and Roman soldiers would begin to desert. The opponents were forced to negotiate. The Parthian leader Phraates IV offered Antony safe passage in return for giving up the siege; Antony responded that he would accept such terms only if the Parthians also returned Ro-

A Roman leader rallies his troops. Antony displayed sincere concern for the legionnaires suffering under his command during his inglorious retreat from Parthia in 36 B.C. But he could not prevent the collapse of discipline among his starving, demoralized ranks.

man prisoners of war and several flags that had been captured. Phraates refused to compromise, and with the onset of winter, Antony was forced to flee without winning his demands.

As Antony's army marched eastward toward Italy, they were not sure whether the Parthians would follow. A Roman soldier who had fought in the region several times before sought an audience with Antony and warned him to expect a Parthian attack as soon as the Romans reached open ground. Two days later, the Romans approached a river whose banks had overflowed. The soldier again issued a warning, saying that the waterway had probably been intentionally flooded by the Parthians as a means of trapping the Romans. He urged his comrades to prepare for battle. But the warning had come too late; as Parthian horsemen descended upon them, thousands of Antony's men were forced into the raging currents and drowned. Antony's only option was to retreat. As usual, he acted quickly and decisively; he ordered the archers, slingers, and dart-throwers to the rear and sides of his retreating column. But with the Parthians in relentless pursuit, disaster was unavoidable.

Each night during the retreat the Parthians hung about like vultures near the Roman camps. By day, Antony's troops were hounded relentlessly, forced almost every mile to crouch down with their shields over their heads to brave an attack. They were overwhelmed by fear. Food was scarce. Several soldiers who sought nourishment in native roots became poisoned and went horribly mad before dying. When they ran out of water and were forced to drink out of local streams, several died from waterborne diseases.

Eventually, as Antony's army faced constant danger and struggle, discipline crumbled. His men began killing each other, vying for what little supplies remained. At one point, Antony's own javelin was stolen. Confusion spread; each man fought to kill or to keep from being killed. It seemed the end had come. Antony, in despair, ordered one of his servants to kill him and cut off his head, so the Parthians could not capture him alive or dishonor his dead body. In his tent, with his friends all weeping around him, Antony readied himself to die by his servant's sword.

And then from the darkness came a salvation so unlikely, so undreamed of, that Antony must have believed he really was being saved by the gods — for who but the gods sent rescue wafting on a breeze? The wind had shifted, and now it carried the smell of the river they had been marching toward, a river the Parthians were known never to cross. The heavenly scent swept through the camp, stopping riot-torn troops in their tracks. Antony's men knew they were saved. When day broke and the Romans reached the riverbank, the Parthians unbent their bows, complimented the Romans on their bravery, and allowed them to pass to the other side.

Six days later the troops reached Armenia, where they knelt and kissed the Roman-ruled earth. In their 27-day ordeal, they had fought 18 battles, losing 24,000 men. Eight thousand more died in snowstorms before they reached the Mediterranean, where Cleopatra met them with clothing and fresh supplies. Antony had lost nearly half his forces and won nothing.

A medallion depicting Cleopatra. After his ignominious defeat in Parthia, Antony joined Cleopatra in Antioch, married her, and returned to Egypt, where he took up permanent residence.

7

The Tragedy of Antony and Cleopatra

News of Antony's disastrous campaign in Parthia did tremendous damage to his political reputation back in Rome. The commoners were further alienated by his decision after the campaign to take up permanent residence in Egypt with Cleopatra. It was learned that Antony had married the Egyptian queen, probably at Antioch in 36 B.C., and that she had given birth to their third child, a son, during the return to Alexandria.

Roman citizens were disturbed by Antony's dalliance with Cleopatra not only because it threatened to undermine Roman imperial power, but also because it was an affront to Roman values — he was forsaking a well-respected Roman woman for an Egyptian temptress. Octavia served as a constant reminder of her husband's offense, living in his house in Rome, taking care of his children, and handling his business affairs. The better she behaved, the worse he looked by comparison.

Octavian capitalized on Antony's waning popularity to increase his own influence in Rome. He constantly spoke out against Antony in the Senate, charging that Antony meant to appropriate the eastern provinces and secede from the Roman Empire,

The love for Cleopatra which now entered his life came as the final and crowning mischief which could befall him.
—PLUTARCH
Roman historian

Sentiments in Rome turned sharply against Antony when it became evident that he planned to shift his seat of power to Egypt. Octavian, who sought to rule Rome by himself, used Antony's dalliance with Cleopatra to incite opposition in the Senate.

95

Cleopatra depicted as a goddess-queen, wearing the helmet of Isis and holding the scepter and ankh (cross) of her pharaonic ancestors. Like her father, Auletes, Cleopatra devoted most of her energies to staving off foreign domination of Egypt.

96

establishing Egypt as the capital of a new independent state and Cleopatra as its goddess-queen. Octavian took two other very important steps in consolidating his power: He won great honors by defeating Pompey the Younger, who had been harassing Roman merchant ships in the Mediterranean, and he managed to get Lepidus officially removed from the Second Triumvirate and sent into exile.

In 34 B.C., Antony had an opportunity to regain some of his lost support. First, he showed surprising talent for organization in restructuring the way Rome's eastern provinces were administered. Then he declared war on Artavasdes — the Armenian king who had deserted Antony's cause during the Parthian campaign — and won a stunning victory. But, instead of bringing Artavasdes as a prisoner to Rome and holding his triumph there, he went to Egypt. During the ceremony celebrating his Armenian campaign, Antony took the opportunity to bestow further honors on his Egyptian wife. Cleopatra was endowed with the title "Queen of Queens," and, along with her son Caesarion (of whom Julius Caesar was the father), she was named ruler of Cyprus, Libya, and Egypt. Antony's three children by Cleopatra — Alexander, Cleopatra, and Helios — were made leaders of Armenia, Media, Cyrene, Syria, and Cilicia. Antony's generous division of his eastern provinces, known to history as the "donations of Alexander," made Roman citizens furious.

Antony also took up the propaganda war with Octavian — whom from the beginning he had expected would try to become sole ruler of Rome. He asserted that Octavian had not divided up the empire fairly and that Octavian had not returned ships lent from Antony's fleet. But simple propaganda could not undo the damage Antony had already done. It could not dispel the notion in most Romans' minds that Antony, in his passion for Cleopatra and entranced with his own image of himself as a god-king beside a goddess-queen, had given Cleopatra what she most desired: the independence of Egypt, the land her ancestors had ruled for centuries. What Antony did not anticipate was how much the Romans

Cleopatra must be judged as destroying Antony's reputation more than almost any factor in the east. Whether or not Cleopatra controlled Antony, people believed she did.
—ELEANOR G. HUZAR
American historian

wanted to keep Egypt and the other lands he had given Cleopatra. From 34–32 B.C., the personal and political rivalry between Antony and Octavian grew increasingly bitter. While Octavian exaggerated the heinousness of Antony's acts to turn Roman feeling against him, Antony remained convinced that Octavian meant to destroy him utterly.

Eventually, the conflict escalated to war. In 32 B.C., when the term of the Second Triumvirate officially ended, Antony divorced Octavia and directed Roman consuls still loyal to him to come to Alexandria. Then he began preparing to fight: He sent 16 legions to the Egyptian seacoast to wait while he amassed money, ships, and supplies. Cleopatra, who contributed a great deal toward the preparations, insisted that she be allowed to fight in the war, too. She feared that if she remained in Egypt, Octavia might take advantage of her absence to get Antony back.

Antony's initial preparations for the war went so well that many of his supporters started celebrating his inevitable victory before the fighting even began. For his part, Octavian was alarmed; in contrast to Antony's swift readiness he was having some trouble raising funds. All over Italy there were complaints about the new, heavier taxes he was levying. Many historians have suggested that had Antony attacked at once, he might have beaten Octavian.

As it turned out, two years passed before they finally faced each other. By that time Octavian had rallied the support of the entire Italian peninsula, whose colonies banded together in an alliance called the *coniuratio Italiae*, and in the most important decision of his career, he chose Agrippa, a naval commander of great skill, to command his fleet. In the Senate, he destroyed what was left of Antony's reputation by reading Antony's will; it stipulated that Antony be buried not in Rome, but in Alexandria, and it bequeathed to Cleopatra all Roman territories in the east. Many populare senators who had previously been ambivalent about opposing a former ally were now firmly committed to Octavian's cause.

By 31 B.C., Antony had amassed a huge force: 800

> *Octavian accused Antony of every immorality, of throwing away Rome's welfare for the eastern harlot queen, of adopting eastern religion and customs . . . every appeal was made to Roman xenophobia and fears of the east to break down Antony's heroic reputation.*
> —ELEANOR G. HUZAR
> American historian

ships and more than 100,000 soldiers. He and Cleopatra had moved this army to the western shore of Greece with the intention of eventually attacking Italy. Meanwhile, in southern Italy, Agrippa had gathered a fleet of 400 ships and an army of 90,000 men. Although from the numbers Antony seemed to have the edge in naval forces, his ships were not as maneuverable as Agrippa's, and his naval crew was less experienced. He had pressed every Greek man and boy into service, but many of the boats still lacked full crews. Antony himself was a land fighter, and so were his Roman soldiers. The men begged him not to crowd his legions onto boats for a sea battle but rather to fight on land where they knew how to win.

But Cleopatra thought otherwise. She urged a naval battle, thinking that yielding the sea to Octavian would be humiliating. Besides, in the back of her mind she was also thinking that if the fight went badly for Antony, she would be better able to escape by boat.

An early Roman ship. After the Senate declared war on Antony in 32 B.C., he and Cleopatra sailed to Greece with a huge armada. Antony had a larger navy than did Octavian, but his vessels were slower, and they were manned by inexperienced crews.

Meanwhile, Agrippa and his forces sailed across the Ionian Sea from Italy. Upon reaching western Greece, they attacked and captured one of Antony's supply depots. Then they interdicted a number of supply ships that had sailed from Egypt. The real purpose was to distract Antony's attention from the advance of Octavian's infantry via a second wave of warships. By the time Antony understood this, Octavian's forces had launched a surprise attack against his main naval headquarters at Actium. Rushing there, Antony found his navy trapped inside the Ambracian Gulf. Soon thereafter, Octavian's land forces appeared from behind a hill overlooking the gulf and completed the blockade of Antony's navy. Antony and Cleopatra were safe, but all their ships were either destroyed or immobilized.

With the approach of summer, Antony's naval soldiers began running out of supplies. Disease was rampant. Some died of malaria and dysentery. Others deserted to the enemy camp. Still, Antony had no desire to surrender; it was only a matter of time, he thought, before his forces broke the blockade.

Marcus Agrippa (center) was chosen by Octavian to command his fleet in the civil war against Antony, which began in Greece in the summer of 31 B.C. Agrippa, a skilled strategist, intercepted Antony's supplies from Egypt and overran several of his land bases.

One August morning it seemed the moment had come. In a fog his best admiral Sosius broke out of the blockade, chasing a group of enemy ships from the entrance to the gulf. But Agrippa was ready for this desperate move and drove Sosius back. By the month's end Antony was restless, wondering if he ought to withdraw with his infantry and abandon the fleet. Perhaps, he thought, he should risk total defeat with an all-out naval attack.

His land commander, Crassus (not related to the member of the First Triumvirate), pressed for a retreat by land. But Cleopatra, whose opinion carried greater weight, still wanted a sea battle. A land march would be too difficult, she argued, for the terrain in Greece was rugged and mountainous. And even if they escaped pursuit by Octavian, she further pointed out, they would be cut off from Egypt, their center of power. Besides, her money and treasure were on board one of the trapped ships; she would not abandon it. Antony was faced with a difficult decision: if he left his fleet now, he might need years to rebuild his naval power. On the other hand, a land march would enable him to gather reinforcements and to regroup for the kind of battle he had a better chance of winning. In fact, cutting his naval losses now seemed altogether the best idea — but it meant leaving Cleopatra, and this he would not do.

He decided to try to break the blockade — to attack Agrippa on the water. And so began the Battle of Actium: On the clear, bright morning of September 2, 31 B.C., Antony sailed toward the mouth of the Ambracian Gulf, leading 230 ships that carried a force of some 20,000 soldiers. His vessels were like floating forts, massive and strong but also clumsy and slow. Fore and aft on each one loomed sturdy towers filled with archers and slingers; on the iron-reinforced decks, soldiers crowded together, sweating in their armor. Below decks, oarsmen, packed 10 rows high, rowed with all their strength. In the middle of the gulf, they spread out in a double line that stretched a mile and a half in either direction. To the right sailed Antony; to the left, Sosius; bringing up the rear was Cleopatra's 60-vessel fleet,

The Roman historian Plutarch credits Agrippa, shown here, with Octavian's final mastery of the Roman world. In the climactic battle of the civil war in September 31 B.C., Agrippa trapped Antony's navy in a bay near Actium.

which included the flagship *Antonias*, upon which she herself sailed with her treasury.

Farther away from shore, Octavian's fleet prepared for action. His armada was twice the size of Antony's, bearing an army of almost 40,000 men. Its vessels were smaller, lighter, and more maneuverable than Antony's. Each carried an ingenious device called a grapnel hook, a gadget developed by Agrippa. Fired from a catapult, the hook tangled the rigging of enemy vessels, rendering their sails useless. With their decks stripped of all extraneous equipment and their heavy sails left on shore, Agrippa's boats waited for Antony's fleet to make its move.

Around noon, Antony made a break for the mouth of the gulf. As he did so, a breeze sprang up — but it was from the wrong direction. The heavy sails on board each of Antony's ships now became a tremendous burden, forcing his oarsmen to row twice as hard. Facing a crisis, Antony directed them to head toward open water to the south where they might evade Agrippa's larger force. But the distinguished admiral gave them no room to escape. Soon many of Antony's battleships were trapped, each surrounded by two or three of Agrippa's speedy little boats. The great catapults on Antony's ships hurled boulders toward their foes. The rival ships locked together, their crews engaged in hand-to-hand combat, battling with swords, daggers, and axes. On the decks of every vessel, showers of arrows buzzed like vicious insects, and blood ran in thick streams.

Eventually, fires broke out on many of Antony's trapped ships, suffocating hundreds of oarsmen where they sat. Attempting to cope with the heat of the conflagrations, some of Antony's men stripped off their armor only to be pierced by enemy arrows. Others jumped overboard, and many drowned. The majority of Antony's ships stood immobile, their oars splintered and broken by Agrippa's men.

Even so, all was not lost. A portion of Antony's ships capitalized on their size and strength to escape disaster. As these ships wheeled around behind Octavian's fleet, they inflicted tremendous damage with their artillery. Antony paced the deck of his ship, directing his men with a fury. Suddenly his attention and that of everyone involved in the fighting was diverted by a spectacular sight on the horizon: Cleopatra's flagship had unfurled its magnificent purple sails. But instead of heading toward the battle, the flagship — in fact all of Cleopatra's Egyptian fleet — was sailing out the mouth of the gulf, back toward Egypt. Antony nearly lost his mind. His queen could not abandon him now. Jumping from his own ship to a smaller, faster vessel, he raced after her. He would follow her all the way to Alexandria, leaving his men to die without their leader.

With the departure of Antony and Cleopatra, the advantage belonged to Agrippa; by nightfall, the battle was over. A few of Antony's ships remained floating on the dark sea, their blackened timbers smoldering silently. The rest had been sunk or captured. More than 5,000 of Antony's men had died.

"Cleopatra's Last Feast," painted in the imaginative 19th-century neoclassical style. After Cleopatra's and Antony's inglorious retreat at Actium, the doomed lovers attempted to numb their defeat and despair with unrepentant extravagance in Alexandria.

Those who survived remained in shock over the desertion of their leader. After arriving in Alexandria, Antony, realizing the enormity of his defeat and the ignominy of his desertion, became horribly despondent. For days he spoke to no one, not even Cleopatra. He began giving away his treasure, spreading it among his friends and even among those who had fought for Octavian. He built himself a tiny house, where for months he lived bitterly and alone. When at last he returned to Cleopatra's palace, the two spent most of their time drinking and feasting, attempting to numb their despair in the face of imminent doom. Octavian was on his way to Egypt.

Knowing that it would be impossible now to fight Octavian, Antony sent messengers to the victorious general, pleading to be allowed to live quietly, without power or fortune, in Egypt. For her part, Cleopatra begged Octavian to allow Egypt to remain independent. But Octavian would not answer Antony and told Cleopatra her only salvation would be to have Antony expelled or put to death. Cleopatra refused.

On the night of August 29, 30 B.C., with Octavian only a few hours away, Antony held a final dinner for his friends. He would, he said, face his enemy as best he could, with the ships and infantry he still possessed. Later, when all had gone sadly to bed, a very strange thing happened: Music, singing, and the joyful shouts of an invisible crowd rose from the darkened streets, a ghostly parade of pleasure moving through the city's center and out the gates. Witnesses to the apparition claimed that it marked the departure of Antony's patron, the god Bacchus, who finally chose to desert his mortal counterpart.

The next morning Antony's few remaining troops also fled, going over to Octavian the moment he appeared in Egypt. Antony rushed back to the palace where Cleopatra had barricaded herself. He was told she had committed suicide. Inconsolable, Antony immediately resolved to follow her into death and stabbed himself near the heart. As it turned out, rumors of Cleopatra's suicide were false. When Cleopatra's servants discovered Antony's dying

Antony now sent Octavius another challenge to meet him in single combat, but all he received was the retort that Antony might find many other ways to end his life.

—PLUTARCH
Roman historian

body, they hauled him by ropes up to her window and pulled him into her room.

Half mad with grief, Cleopatra laid him upon her own bed and tore her clothes and smeared her face with his blood in her terrible distress. All their adventures, their triumphs, and the love she truly felt for him made her ambitions and schemes seem like nothing now that he was dying. He tried to calm her, asking for some wine. Then he told her not to grieve but to remember the joy they had shared, and how happy she had always made him, and how he loved her.

And then he died. He was 51. In his busy life, he had enjoyed the happiest adventures and triumphs, suffered the worst possible sorrows and defeats, and known the deepest love. He had risked all, lost all — and he was gone.

In the following days, Octavian and his messengers visited Cleopatra, trying to persuade her that

Cleopatra wails over the body of Antony, declaring, in Shakespeare's words, "So it should be, that none but Antony/Should conquer Antony/but woe 'tis so!" His suicide had been triggered by a false rumor of Cleopatra's death.

Octavian took the name Caesar Augustus on becoming
the first emperor of the Roman Empire. He undertook
enormous feats of governmental reorganization during
his just and admirable 45-year rule.

they meant her no harm. But she knew Octavian's plan: to take her back to Rome and parade her in shame before people who hated her. To escape this humiliation, it is said that she had a servant bring her an asp, a poisonous snake that she let bite her. Dead at the age of 39, she was buried next to Antony.

So the Roman strongman and his Egyptian queen passed out of this life and into history together, and Octavian, now called Augustus Caesar, went on to become the first and one of the greatest of the Roman emperors. With the Battle of Actium, the Roman Republic had ended and the Roman Empire had begun, to continue in power for many hundreds of years. But although Octavian won and Antony went down to defeat, the life of the latter continues to capture our imaginations. For in identifying himself with his gods, he illuminated his nature as a man, exposing his best virtues and most tragic flaws — and with them, our own. He did not always win, yet he always tried; he did not always behave as a hero, yet he had a hero's heart. He was not afraid to fight or to love, although his love at last ruined him. Two thousand years after he lived and died, we still remember Marc Antony.

"The Death of Cleopatra," by Guercino. The poisonous asp that, according to legend, Cleopatra chose for her suicide had special significance: The emblem of Egypt's royal family was a viper curled into the shape of a crown.

107

Further Reading

Bradford, Ernle. *Julius Caesar: The Pursuit of Power.* New York: William Morrow, 1984.

Bruns, Roger. *Julius Caesar.* New York: Chelsea House Publishers, 1987.

Carcopino, Jerome. *Daily Life in Ancient Rome.* New Haven: Yale University Press, 1958.

Grant, Michael. *History of Rome.* New York: Scribners, 1978.

Hoobler, Dorothy, and Thomas Hoobler. *Cleopatra.* New York: Chelsea House Publishers, 1986.

Huzar, Eleanor Goltz. *Mark Antony: A Biography.* Minneapolis: University of Minnesota Press, 1978.

Perowne, Stewart. *Death of the Roman Republic.* Garden City, NY: Doubleday, 1968.

Plutarch. *Plutarch's Lives.* New York: Modern Library, 1967.

Starr, Chester G. *The Ancient Romans.* New York: Oxford University Press, 1971.

Chronology

Index

Mary Kittredge, an award-winning writer of fiction and nonfiction, was born in 1949 in Pewaukee, Wisconsin. She is the coauthor of *The Electronic Money Machine: Profits From Your Home Computer.* Her recent novels are *The Shelter* (with Kevin O'Donnell, Jr.) and *Murder in Mendocino.* She is also the author of FREDERICK THE GREAT in the Chelsea House series WORLD LEADERS   PAST & PRESENT.

Arthur M. Schlesinger, jr., taught history at Harvard for many years and is currently Albert Schweitzer Professor of the Humanities at City University of New York. He is the author of numerous highly praised works in American history and has twice been awarded the Pulitzer Prize. He served in the White House as special assistant to Presidents Kennedy and Johnson.
